The Healing Oasis

Meditations
for Mind, Body, and Spirit

by
Sharon Moon

UNITED CHURCH PUBLISHING HOUSE

The Healing Oasis:
Meditations for Mind, Body, and Spirit

Canadian Cataloguing in Publication Data

Moon, Sharon, 1945-
   The healing oasis : meditations for mind, body, and spirit

Includes bibliographical references and index
ISBN 1-55134-084-4

1. Meditations. I. Title.

BV4832.2.M66 1998   242   C98-930851-0

United Church Publishing House
3250 Bloor Street West, Fourth Floor
Etobicoke, Ontario
Canada M8X 2Y4
416-231-5931
bookpub@uccan.org

  2 3 4 5   03 02 01 00 99 98

Design and Production: Department of Publishing and Graphics
Cover Image: *Green Star* by Simon Andrew

Printed in Canada

 980415

CONTENTS

FOREWORD

Healing Oasis: Meditations for Mind, Body, and Spirit is a welcome gift from the life experiences of my friend, Sharon Moon. I have often thought that Sharon should be called "Sharing Moon" because she shares her gifts so generously with others and in so doing also shares her light, a light that shines like the moon in the darkest night.

I can personally vouch for the healing power embedded in her meditations. When I was in a long and painful stage in my journey with cancer, it was Sharon who brought the gift of healing into my home and my heart by guiding me through the dying parts of my spiritual restlessness to a place of light and hope. Now others beyond the circle of her own congregation and her circle of friends have an opportunity to experience that same healing for body, mind, and spirit.

This book has at least four special strengths that make it rise above other books on spirituality. First, it accepts people where they are and leads them where they need to be in their faith journey. It does not assume that everyone will have the same experience or grow in the same way. It gives permission for participants to opt out at any stage where the journey becomes too painful, and at the same time encourages them to begin the journey again when they are ready.

Second, it does not, like so many books on feminist spirituality, assume that all of those who are making the journey are women. Although the book is cast within a feminist framework, the material in this book has been developed and used in groups of men and women, acknowledging that both women and men need to grow in new directions.

Third, while rooted in scripture it goes far beyond the traditional Bible study. It does not stop at asking what we think about the passages or what they mean; it gently probes our feelings and calls to our spirits, making it truly a resource for body, mind, and spirit.

Fourth, it does not leave us luxuriating in personal well-being; it is transformative growth and self-development with a purpose, calling us to live the justice of the gospel in the world.

For this, God bless you Sharon.

Dr. Anne Squire

PREFACE

———◆•◆•◆———

This resource will help those who want to gain confidence and skill in leading guided imagery meditations in groups. It is also for those wishing to use meditation for their personal healing journey. The book begins with a general introduction to the power of meditation in healing, spiritual integration, and community spiritual development. There follows background and guidance for those who wish to use meditation for group work.

Where the resource is being used for individual reflection, the reader may wish to skip over parts of the section for group leaders; however, the sections in Part I on introducing and experiencing the guided imagery section of the meditation would be of interest for individual users.

The particular meditations included here are but a sampling of the kinds of meditation we have used in our community. They have been divided into two general areas, Meditations for Healing and Forgiveness and Meditations for Growth and Strength. I would hope that those who become comfortable leading these meditations will want to go on to develop their own meditation experiences.

ACKNOWLEDGEMENTS

———◆·◆·◆———

I wish to thank the congregation of First United Church, Ottawa, for the opportunity I have had to learn and grow in leading meditation in that very stimulating
congregation. This community has taught me more than I can ever imagine about
ministry and spiritual journey. I thank them also for sabbatical times during
which I worked on this resource, and for their receptivity to exploring the spiritual
path with me.

I would like to thank all who have been part of preparing this material for
publication: members of the meditation group who have been its source, those
who have waded through the manuscripts and offered suggestions, encouragement and other support—Howard Clark, Anne Squire, Darla Sloan, Denis Fortin,
Ellie Barrington, and Dima Dupéré. Thanks as well to the United Church Publishing House for editorial support.

Thanks also to my children, Christopher and Jonathan Sims, who have put
up with a preoccupied mother during manuscript preparation; to my stepson,
Simon Andrew, for the painting, called *Green Star*, that appears on the cover.

I wish the blessings of the Spirit on all who use these meditations, whether it be for
their own healing and growth, or for use in groups in community.

PART I

Guidance for those Leading Meditation

CHAPTER

1

THE SPIRIT WELLING UP
IN AN INNER-CITY COMMUNITY

This resource came to birth out of the experience of using guided imagery meditation for thirteen years in my home congregation, First United Church in downtown Ottawa. At first, we discovered that meditation was important not only for
personal spiritual growth and healing, but when shared in a group, it created a
powerful experience of a sustaining, healing community. Our meditation group
provided a base of support for the spiritual journeys of the participants, for their
struggle of daily living, and for the social justice work in which many of our
members were involved.

We began to use guided imagery in the congregation in response to some
particular needs that came to our attention from both inside and outside our
congregation. From the community, we had a specific request for spiritual support
for front-line workers at a downtown food bank. Volunteers felt drained by the
results of fiscal restraint and harsh economic and political policies. For those on
the front lines, policy decisions around social assistance were not just a matter for
theoretical discussion. Day in and day out they were dealing directly with the
people affected by those policies. As they encountered clients with needs beyond
their capacity to meet, the volunteers felt powerless, and spiritually drained.

These food-bank volunteers bore the alienation of working with a group
largely invisible to most of society. In addition, many found that even people in
their own churches were not interested in hearing about the existence of poverty.
When volunteers tried to talk with those who had not experienced this reality they
ran into attitudes of denial and blaming the victim. These combined stresses left
volunteers de-energized, somewhat isolated, and in need of sustenance themselves.

At the same time, there were people in our own congregation longing for community and seeking the kind of spirituality that could help them deal with the very real issues in their lives — spiritual hunger, recovery, vocation, healing, parenting, ageing, illness, meaning, relationships, etc.

We began a six-week experiment in using guided imagery meditation and community sharing to see if this would meet some of these diverse needs. This group lasted *not six weeks, but eleven years.* The group operated as an open group; so many people came and went over those years. All those who participated helped form the experience and learning that I share with you here.

Some went on to other communities and started meditation groups because they valued the experience we shared. Always they came back asking for resources for their work. We searched for materials, but we found very few. Usually those available were not written with groups in mind; or they were by and for Roman Catholic contemplatives focusing only on the individual spiritual journey; or they were written by New Age writers who did not tap into the rich source of images in the scripture and the Christian story.[1] Sometimes the theology in them was not congruent with our own inclusive approach.

HOW MEDITATION HAS AFFECTED PEOPLE IN OUR COMMUNITY

Meditation has been a transforming, healing experience for many who came to our group. Some have said that it was the first time that scripture had touched them. The Bible had seemed alien, something from a remote and largely irrelevant past. Some who came were seekers looking for a way to connect with their spiritual side. Some were going through a crisis in their lives and felt there was a big hole where God should be. Others had been long-time church members, but the busyness of being part of a church community threatened to cut them off from the living water of God's Spirit. Some who came had destructive experiences with ways of using scripture that were abusive and guilt-producing. Women, men, gays, lesbians, professionals, unemployed, those dealing with addictions of many sorts, those who had suffered abuse — all found they could come together in a spiritual community that was a source of healing and empowerment; all found a place where they could share their real concerns, and the struggles and joys of the journey, in a context of spiritual openness and seeking.

CONGREGATIONAL DEVELOPMENT AND GROWTH

When we began the meditation group, we thought it would primarily meet individual spiritual growth and support needs. An unanticipated and delightful outcome has been the congregational growth and deepening that developed as a result of our group. People came with diverse needs at different times of their lives. Some came when they had a real need, others came seeking deeper growth. Many who came to the meditation group would otherwise never darken the doorway of organized religion. It was an introduction to Christian community that enabled many people to join the "upstairs church" as we often called Sunday worship.

Over a period of time, the personality of our congregation was affected by the widening pool of people who believed they had experiential, living access to the Spirit. This group of people have moved into leadership roles on the Session (Eldership), the Pastoral Care, Worship and Christian Development Committees, and have become involved in Sunday School teaching, small-group leadership, choir, etc. They brought to these new involvements their valuing of the Spirit, and their desire to discern the spiritual path in decision making.

The effect of the group has spilled over into all areas of our congregational life. It has meant that we have a large number of people who feel comfortable talking about their faith and how it relates to their daily lives, and who are willing to lead worship. They feel comfortable dialoguing with scripture and spiritual values and experience. It has also deepened the spiritual depth of many who offer pastoral care in our congregation.

Meditation has interacted with our worship life as well. We have often used guided imagery meditation in place of a sermon. It has been used at many healing services. It has deepened the spiritual path for our community as a whole, and been formative in the character and spirit of our community.

Because of the power of the experience at First, which stretched and deepened, sustained and strengthened those who came to the group, I wanted to offer these experiences for the use of other communities.

USING THESE MEDITATIONS IN YOUR OWN CONGREGATION

At First, we have used meditation in a number of contexts. You may find these meditations useful in a healing service, as a sermon during regular worship, at a retreat or workshop, as worship at a meeting, or in groups for personal growth or prayer. These meditations are good tools for teaching prayer and spiritual reflection with people of all ages. Some can be adapted (usually shortened and made more concrete) for use with children. Our youth group finds that meditation is a spiritual experience they can relate to.

The meditations can be used by pastoral care visitors with people living with anxiety, illness, grief, or chronic pain. The resource could also be offered as a gift to someone living with chronic illness or pain, physical or emotional illness, or struggling with grief. While they are not meant, in any way, to replace scientific medical treatment, the healing meditations can work *with* various treatments to strengthen and encourage healing, recovery, and wellness. I have used the healing meditations with people undergoing cancer treatment or various treatments for HIV. I have also based small-group rituals of healing for survivors around some of the meditations.

2

YEARNING FOR LIVING WATER
IN WILDERNESS TIMES

In these supposedly secular times there is a deep yearning for the sacred. Bookstores are full of books on spirituality, such as the instant best-sellers *Care of the Soul* and *Soul Mates* by Thomas Moore, *The Road Less Traveled* by Scott Peck, and *The Celestine Prophecy* by James Redfield. The spiritual thirst that is at the heart of our age is found both inside and outside traditional church communities. People want, not just to *talk about* God, but to *experience* the sacred in the midst of frequently chaotic, rapidly changing lives.

As a minister in an active inner-city congregation, I often encounter this profound desire for a spirituality that activates the sometimes dormant inner life. We, like many congregations, are constantly having people come to taste and see what our congregation and faith are about. People come wanting to know God and to awaken their awareness of the presence of God. Yet many who come seeking are sceptical of traditional Christian teaching. As they have encountered the tradition, some have been wounded by experiences that left them feeling guilty, ashamed, or disempowered. They may have found stones, not bread, in the past. And so it is understandable that many people are more willing to look outside the Christian tradition for spirituality.

I work with a community of people committed to justice and healing work, who treasure spiritual growth and searching. Just as in Jesus' day, many of the people attracted to the gospel and to the faith community come from the edges of the culture and some come in need of personal healing. My own personal spiritual need, as well as the need of the people I serve, is for concrete practices that nurture and sustain a spirituality that is inclusive and non-hierarchical; one that values not only thinking and analysis, but also experience, intuition, and imagination.

This period of history is one that is dislocating for many people. Even if one is not aware of quantum physics, or chaos theory, there is a sense of dislocation and change in the air; the very nature of how we view reality is shifting. Paradigms — those fundamental patterns of thinking and ordering of our reality — are shifting all the time: how we define ourselves in relation to each other and to creation; how we think of work/family relationships; how we think of mind/body, and energy, are all in a period of transformation. Some of us would want to return to the good old days, but for most this is not a viable option.

The people who come to our church are very much affected by these changes, whether consciously or not. They are intelligent people, searching for spiritual paths that are congruent with, and make some sense of, the world that they experience. Christian spiritual paths that might reach into the souls of such people need to be life-enhancing, empowering, and integrated. These paths need to help people reflect deeply on the meaning of life. A spirituality still rooted in a hierarchical, triumphalistic, Christendom culture will reach a limited, ageing population.

At First, we wanted to offer to our community spiritual-growth practices that take scripture seriously, but not literally, and that tap into the mythic power of scriptural symbols. We wanted to offer practices that strengthened people for living their faith in their daily lives. In ministry with both those inside the church and those who come tentatively seeking the Spirit, we have found meditation to be a powerful tool to nourish souls and to heighten awareness of the healing, empowering spirit of God.

THE HEALING OF
WOUNDED SPIRITUAL HISTORIES

Many of us have grown up with a western world-view embedded in rationality and either/or thinking. The traditional theology that emerged in this era has split the spirit and the body into opposites, and labelled one good, and the other evil; one masculine, and the other feminine. There is much recent literature analyzing and attempting to come to grips with the effects of this split. In the church it has resulted in valuing theological analysis and distrusting experience; in valuing thought and rationality over emotion, intuition, creativity, and imagination.

As a theology rooted in this kind of thinking has been put into practice, it has resulted in a disembodied spirituality and a distrust of the body-self. There are still those who shudder at the notion of liturgical dance or body movement in prayer. Historically, it has led to the notion that men — who are more identified with spirit in this way of thinking — are to lead, to *do* the theology, and women — and women's experience of spirit — are to be distrusted at best, and feared as contamination at worst. It has led to an attitude that the Earth (characterized as feminine) is to be subdued or acted upon as something outside us, rather than to an awareness that we are an integral part of the created order.

We desperately need spiritual paths in Christianity that will heal these splits and lead to integration and wholeness. We need this not just for the good of the individual; we need it if we are to survive as a species, at home with Mother Earth. We need to create paths and practices that allow God the space to BE, in ways that God chooses, rather than in ways we control. In the church, I believe, we need to move beyond analytical doctrinal statements, as meaningful as they may be for some, to the experience of the Source of those statements, and we need to help people enter this experience. Otherwise the words we say, no matter how powerful they were to those who originally wrote them, will have no meaning.

Meditation is one among several spiritual disciplines that can help us dip back into the healing, life-giving waters, of the Spirit.[2] Meditation connects us with the eternal, indestructible core of our beings, with our Christ-self. It helps to heal the fundamental wound between the soul and the personality. With practice, meditation can help put us in touch with an inner power for healing and growth, with what Jung called the "Self," and what others have called the soul-self, the God-self, the Christ-within, the core-self, or the Holy Ground of our Being. In this centre we are most fully "ourselves," yet we know by experience our connection to all creation and with the Creator.

THE CARE OF SOUL WOUNDS

Many in our culture live daily with incredible amounts of stress. This stress comes from many sources, external as well as internal. Often life is a tightly packed series of experiences, one thing after the other. There is little time to reflect, to savour, or to unpack meaning. We are so busy trying to handle "life," responding to all its demands and challenges, that we push down and deny our own heart's desires, and our own deepest longings. At a certain level, we are so out of touch with them, we have even lost the awareness that we have a right to feel them.

Particularly painful experiences get denied as not important enough to worry about, or simply not urgent enough to break through the heavy agenda of "now" demands. A protective wall goes around our deepest core cutting off access to our own centre. We experience a profound loneliness that some try to fill up with doing, with buying, with people, with an addictive seeking for peace "out there." But this loneliness is a spiritual one. The desire to come home to the depths of our own soul-self will not be satisfied by these other attempts to take away the angst. At best they give only momentary respite.

When we spend all our energy outside, we lose contact with our inner spiritual core, with our depths where we could encounter God's truth already planted in us. Taking space and time for meditation helps us find our centre. We find the place to be still, and to know that God is here.

For many, perhaps most of us, from early in our lives, we have become estranged from our deepest, truest, sacred selves. In the process of growing up, our personalities have had to adapt to the demands of the "real" external world, building up a false-self to meet life. This manifests as a feeling of spiritual emptiness. Even for those of us who seem to have everything, there is often a strong sense that something is missing. We are left with a deep soul wound. We thirst for something more; more depth in relationships with God, with others, with the self. It is as if we know, in some part of our being, that we were not meant to live this way. It is as if in our souls, we know that isolation, abandonment, loneliness, and injustice are not what we are created for.

Meditation is one path that helps us be in touch with the inner world, helps us centre, and focus and value our soul-self. In this relaxed, surrendered soul place, we can heighten our awareness of God's presence as it bathes us with healing energy, and renews us with courage and insight for the journey.

THE THIRST FOR COMMUNITY

In our North American context, there is a desire for communion, for community. The church *should* be a perfect place for people to come together to connect with meaning beyond themselves. It should be a place to be grasped by a vision that is life-giving, and empowers people to live, fully alive to the Spirit. Yet for many people who go to church seeking to fill this thirst, public worship on Sunday morning does not satisfy the yearning. Words fill the space that was longing for silence, for reflection, for just "being" in the presence of God and God's people. The theology expressed in worship sometimes feels alienating, guilt producing, disempowering. It can feel as if God is more talked "about" than communed "with." And even in churches deeply concerned with the state of the world, one can end up feeling more guilty, powerless, hopeless, and paralyzed on leaving worship than when one entered.

Some seekers of faith feel that part of them would not be welcome in church: the part that questions and doubts, the part that struggles and is angry, the part that is wounded and feels anxiety, the part that desires and dreams and envisions a different way of living. What happens all too often is that people stop going, writing church off as irrelevant to their lives. Sometimes they continue to attend, but bring to worship only the parts they think will be "acceptable" in church. It is even more tragic when they feel that *God* can receive only certain "acceptable" aspects of themselves. When this happens, the church, the individual, and God all get short-changed.

The meditation group in our congregation became a powerful place for people to break down these barriers to their spiritual development. As those who attended allowed God to be present to their whole being, many experienced a living water of grace that truly amazed them and transformed their lives. As they met other members of our congregation who were also searching, and being real with God, a number of people felt drawn into the larger life and work of the congregation as well. Some were able to encounter, for the first time ever, the healing experience of being beloved of God. They discovered that their lives had meaning and greater depth as they became responsive to the experience of the Holy.

THE THIRST FOR JUSTICE

Like those food bank workers who approached First United looking for their own sustenance, being a person with a passion for justice can be very difficult, especially in reactionary times. Social justice work, measured only in terms of results, can be very depressing and de-energizing. Activism, if it is simply reactive, can be like spinning wheels; expending incredible amounts of energy, but not moving ahead. Activists have a special need to develop spirituality for the long haul in the struggle for justice. Diving deeply into the pool of the grace and renewing power of the Spirit provides the strength to continue the struggle.

Christians are people who are willing and able to sustain a tough, resilient hope and have done so, sometimes against terrible odds, for two thousand years. We need nourishment from a vision of justice that comes not from some external political persuasion, but rather from the heart and soul of a just and loving God. In this way we can avoid burn out and disillusionment.

Meditation is one tool that can help nurture the spiritual roots of justice tempered with compassion. Those who practise meditation over a period of time can actually become more alive to and aware of life around them. And so a practice that, on the surface, may look like a very internal, private one, can lead to deeper engagement in grappling with the pain and suffering of the world, as well as the strength to grapple.

Those who do justice work out of a deep well of spirituality draw others to the work. Action that is coupled with discerned spiritually is likely to be less reactive, more centred, more clear, more grounded. This helps to make it more sustainable and resilient in tough times.

CHAPTER

3

———◆◆◆———

MEDITATION AS A LIFE-GIVING SOURCE

AN ANCIENT ART MADE NEW

Meditation has a long history as a spiritual discipline in many religious expressions, including the Christian tradition. Many in the West are more familiar with eastern forms of meditation, such as Yoga, Zen, Tibbetan Buddhism, or others. However Christianity, both eastern and western, has a rich heritage of meditation practice as well.[3]

In the Christian tradition there are two major schools of meditation both rooted in a world-view that values both physical and spiritual realities. Both are counter to the Aristotelian world-view that denies any connection between the physical and spiritual world; a view that has predominated in the West since late medieval times. The gulf between the physical and spiritual worlds became further widened in the eighteenth and nineteenth centuries through the Enlightenment and Newtonian science. The material world that can be accessed and analyzed through the five senses came to be seen as what constitutes reality. The importance and reality of the spiritual world was ignored or even mocked.

In the twentieth century, as we have come to recognize the limitations of rational materialism, we are rediscovering ancient traditions in all world religions, and in Aboriginal tradition, that are rooted in a much more holistic world-view that values the spiritual. Christianity too is rediscovering the spiritual wisdom of its ancient traditions in meditative practice.

There are two main schools in Christian tradition. One tradition, called *apophatic* (from the Greek, meaning "without images") has roots as far back as the Desert Fathers and Mothers who lived in the Egyptian desert during the fourth and fifth centuries. After the persecutions of the early church ceased, these early

Christians searched for a new form of costly discipleship. They went into the desert to escape conforming to the values of the world, and became ascetic spiritual leaders. Their prayer was one of silence, of solitude, of praying without ceasing, of emptying, of losing self.

The Desert Fathers and Mothers wanted to experience the deep wisdom of divine silence that unmasks illusions about ourselves and about God, and to speak out of this silence to the needs of people. When asked how to pray, they suggested simple prayer, repeated ceaslessly, a mantra-like repetition of a scripture or simple phrase in prayer.

What has come to be known as the Jesus Prayer of the Desert Fathers was rediscovered by a Russian peasant in Eastern Europe many centuries later. It was simply "Lord Jesus have mercy," prayed ceaslessly until the prayer and the person praying become one.[4]

In Canada in 1977, Dom John Mains, a Benedictine priest, founded a small religious community in Montreal that has reawakened the practice of silent mantra meditation in groups. Christian meditation groups have sprung up in much of Canada, and in other parts of the world as a result of his teachings.[5]

A second type of Christian meditation is called *ketaphatic* (from the Greek, meaning "with images"). This has been the practice of much of the Christian tradition, and involves the meditator using active imagination, visualization, and symbol after a period of relaxation and focusing. Ignatius of Loyola collected the spiritual devotional exercises that were practised in medieval monasteries into a book called *Spiritual Exercises*. These exercises use images and imagination to invite meditators to step into the biblical narrative, to enter into the experiences described in scripture, to meet Jesus on the streets of Palestine as he heals and teaches, to walk with him as he goes to cross.

Despite some of their dated cultural and theological interpretations, the *Spiritual Exercises* still provides an excellent description of the techniques and process used for meditation of scripture in this tradition. This imaginative communion with Jesus has led many to genuine spiritual encounter. It created a renewal movement within Christianity in the sixteenth century, and has been widely used by the Jesuit order that St. Ignatius founded. Christians since that time have practised this type of imaginative praying.

Both *apophatic* and *ketaphatic* traditions are of great value and will appeal to different personalities, or to the same person for different types of spiritual needs. This resource uses imagery meditation in the Ignatian tradition. However the early part of each meditation is a period of relaxing, centering, clearing, silencing, and letting go, as the Desert Fathers and Mothers may have done.

VISUALIZATION:
A PATH OF HEALING INTEGRATION

The value of meditation is recognized in areas other than religion as well. It is used in some therapies, e.g., Jungian, Gestalt, feminist, neurolinguistic programming, and psychosynthesis, because it is believed to have healing, integrative power. It accesses the unconscious mind, which has incredible powers, to create healing and change.

Visualization is always going on in our minds, awake and asleep. The pictures in our mind affect our bodily reactions, our emotions, and even our actions. To test this out, I invite you to imagine a juicy fresh-cut orange; let yourself imagine the smell of the orange, the taste of its sweet juice. Probably your mouth begins to water, and you can almost smell the orange in the air. Now, let yourself imagine something that frightens you. For me it would be a big bat flying about or perhaps a squirming snake. Notice what happens in your emotions and body.

Visualization is powerful, and it goes on whether we are conscious of it or not. Sometimes the pictures stored in our minds are life-giving, and help us to live more fully. Sometimes we have a negative image that we keep replaying in our minds long after the event has passed. This causes us to experience the painful experience again and again, reinforcing victimization and negative patterns of thinking. Eventually we discover that our emotional life, and even our physical life is being affected.

If the images and messages planted in our unconscious mind suggest that we are not worthwhile, not loveable, not worthy of God's care or concern, then our physical and emotional well-being are affected, and our relationship with God will be distorted. As a minister I can tell a person that God loves them, but there is power of a whole different order when the person can have direct experience of that love through meditation.

Visualization in meditation accesses the unconscious, allowing transformation to occur. It can help clear out negative pictures, stored from the past, and allow the possibility of positive life-affirming ones to be planted. It can give new vision.

There are those in the medical profession, concerned with mind-body connections in the healing of illness, who use meditation widely. It has been shown to have a powerful effect in activating and supporting the healing power we all have within us.[6] Many involved in personal growth and spiritual development have found imagery meditation to be an important tool. It is used in many alternative healing traditions. Meditation and visualization are even used in sports, recognizing that they are important tools in actually changing what an athlete can do.

ENCOUNTERING SCRIPTURE

Meditation is a powerful means of encountering scripture, both for those who know their Bible so well that the stories have lost any capability to move them, and for those who are just beginning to crack the cover on their Bibles. Scripture is a treasure trove of spiritual wisdom in images and symbols. Biblical images and symbols are archetypal. They touch into the core of the human condition. Carl Jung has helped us to realize the power of symbols, explaining that symbols lead more directly to the experience of the "thing itself," than do "words about," or analysis.[7] They point to and give direct access to what lies behind the symbols. This should hardly come as a surprise to religious people who have regular experience of the power and multi-layered meaning of sacraments such as communion and baptism.

If we allow scripture to touch only our conscious, rational minds, we are cut off from accessing the largest part of ourselves, the unconscious. In meditation we integrate symbols and enter images of scripture allowing us to connect deeply with the vast reservoir of inner wisdom that is in the unconscious. Sometimes, in meditation, we enter the biblical scene directly to imagine what might have been happening then. When we do this, it is not only for the purpose of recreating the past; but also to experience the spiritual dynamics and transformation of the participants in the story. This allows us to *become* the story. This experience can allow us to look at our own life differently. At other times, we can allow the images to unfold their wisdom for us in our current situation. In meditation, we move experientially into scripture rather than talk "about" it from outside. For many in our group, this approach to scripture awakened a desire to learn more about this book that still had the power to change lives.

REACTIVATING IMAGINATION

Most of us have had our imaginative sides thwarted during childhood. We have generally accepted the cultural view that creativity and imagination are a childish waste of time. Outward concrete achievement, particularly if it is monetarily rewarded, is what is real and of value. These cultural values have also seeped into our church and spiritual practice. It may be true that prayer has at times been used in Christian history as a way to avoid life, to spiritualize the painful reality of living, and thus to deny the need for change. However, an outward focus, that denies the inner journey, is also alienating. It causes us to distrust and to devalue the inner journey and the incredible power for transformation and action that is possible there.

Meditation helps integrate imagination and feeling. It values symbol and image and the personal experience of the meditator. A meditator can practise and become more focused and disciplined in meditation, but no one else can be an "expert" on another's experience of meditation. Because of the focus on relaxation, breathing, and body awareness, meditation helps integrate the body in spirituality. Meditation is a way of moving from left-brain thinking, which is analytical, logical, and linear, to right-brain thinking, which is imaginative, intuitive, integrative, and creative. We need to develop this unvalued side of our being to provide the balance and wholeness that we need as individuals, and as a culture and a church.

PERSONAL SPIRITUAL TRANSFORMATION

In meditation, we move into the world of poetry and symbol. We move out of the linear, logical, rational, thinking world into a world of intuition, where truth presents itself in a flash of insight, in an image, a symbol, or a phrase. These insights may be momentary, but they connect with meaning. They can cause profound changes in our inner world, and in the way we respond to and experience our outer world. They can impart a kind of "gut" knowing, difficult to put into words, but which has the power to transform the meditator. They can change the perspective one has on the self, but also the perspective one has on scripture and on God. They can change how one sees the outer world and cause deep lasting shifts in one's emotional condition, in one's mental condition, and in one's capacity to see into the heart of things, to feel the texture of life, to experience the joy and pain of others and of the earth. This experience can lead to profound conversion, to deep changes in the way one chooses to live out one's life. Meditation in our culture may be dismissed as "wasting time," as "playing," as "doing nothing," however, it has great power for transformation.

Imagination, when we allow it to be activated, makes us more open, more able to be the "child" we need to be to experience the reign of God in our midst. It helps us to discern where God's Spirit is active in our own situations. For some of our participants, it was in depth meditation that they were able, for the first time, to experience themselves as beloved of God and to experience grace.

As we ground ourselves in God's grace, we have a far greater sense of being at home in the self and at home in an abundant, grace-filled universe. Our sense of self-worth comes into balance. We know ourselves to be a "temple in which the sacred dwells." The ego-self, connected with our personality, can gradually be transformed by the sacred-self. Meditation can lead to a profound celebration of being-ness and of creation.

This celebration of life is transformative, in a culture that too often erodes self-worth and dishonours the sacred dimension of life. Because of this sense of connection with life within and outside ourselves, we can find courage, strength, and clarity to make necessary changes in our own lives and in our world. By practising the presence of God in meditation, we find ourselves more awakened to nudges of the Spirit in our day to day activities and contacts. The inner world and the outer world begin to move towards harmony.

Meditation, rather than taking us "out of the world" and its problems, in fact enhances our capacity to be "in the world," and to feel centred enough to find the courage to act. It can help us have a more holistic stance from which to relate to the world.

USING GUIDED MEDITATION FOR PERSONAL GROWTH

To use the meditations for your own personal quiet time, look at the suggested programme outline in Chapter 5 before you begin. You might wish to put the meditation on tape for your own use. If you do this, read it slowly, giving yourself lots of spaces for reflection. You might want to do some of the suggested gathering exercises. I usually begin with a simple discipline like lighting a candle, taking silence to create space to receive, offering a simple prayer of invocation, inviting wisdom and insight in the time of prayer. Some people like to set a timer so that they will not have to be anxious about how much time is passing while they are in meditation.

Read the scripture (sometimes I do this aloud), noticing anything that seems to connect with you. Our feelings and our intuitions are often neglected ways for us to enter into connection with scripture. Is there one word, or phrase, or insight that is evocative for you at this time? This may draw you; it may be something you notice for the first time or with fresh eyes. It may also be something that confuses you or disturbs you. Pay attention and listen to discern any meaning for you. Then making sure that you are in a comfortable position, with your spine in a straight line, begin the meditation.

Know that you are always free in a meditation. God respects that freedom, and your own pace and response. If ever you find painful memories, growing discomfort, or anxiety that you are not ready to deal with surfacing, give yourself permission to draw away from the meditation. There is no "right" way to do meditation. It may be that you will be invited to return to that place at another time, or it may be that you process the feelings in a different context. It is important to honour your own feelings. Do not work too hard to make things happen. If there are defences that arise, simply be aware of them. Do not do spiritual violence to yourself or allow the meditation to take you where you do not want to go. When I feel overwhelmed by wounded-ness that is too raw to deal with at the moment, I find it useful to image an all-loving Christ or another image of Sacred Presence with me.

When you come out of the meditation, it is important to do so gently and respectfully. It is also useful to spend some time debriefing yourself about what happened. This can be done in a journal or by just reflecting, in a conscious way, about what it might mean for your life. If you notice your inner "judge" rising up to be critical, know that this is not from the Holy, and is only part of your wounded-self, feeling threatened by the possibility of change and of healing. Invite the Healing God to be present to that part of yourself, so that you can embrace what God would give you.

Close with a moment of thankfulness in whatever way makes sense for you. You may wish to share meditation experiences with a trusted friend or spiritual guide, but make sure that this is someone who can really hear you and honour your experience. It is not helpful to share with someone who is interested in "interpreting" your meditation through their own agenda. Remember, that you are always the expert on your own experience. By trusting that experience, and your growing relationship with God, you will experience transformation and healing. It may not always be in ways that you expected, so be prepared for surprises from the God who is always doing something new in our midst.

CHAPTER

4

USING GUIDED IMAGERY IN GROUPS
BACKGROUND FOR LEADERS

OVERCOMING DISCOMFORT WITH SHARING SPIRITUAL EXPERIENCE

In the church in which I grew up, we did not talk about spiritual life. We took literally the scripture suggesting that we were not to display our prayer life in public on street corners. Instead, as we thought scripture told us, we were to go in secret, even into a closet, to meet our God. Jesus had addressed these words to spiritually arrogant people, to those who felt that they had God in their pockets. My experience in church leads me to believe that there is a different problem in mainline congregations today. I see the problem of low self-esteem in matters of the Spirit. Too often people feel that their experiences of God are not worth sharing because they seem so ordinary and unworthy of attention.

Theology and spiritual journey have been given over to professionals. In creating a hierarchy of those "theologically trained" and those "done unto," we lose the insights of the whole community, and the power to be a people of God. Any pastor who shares deeply in the life of the people can tell many stories of encountering the Spirit of God in those who felt they were not "good enough" to be part of God's family. When we do not trust or value our experience of Spirit, we do not share these experiences with others. This means that the community is not nurtured by stories of experiences of God. Using guided imagery meditation creates a space that breaks down these barriers and offers a vehicle for sharing sacred experience.

Many who have come to our meditation group, have said that there is no-where else in their lives that they are able to talk about their spiritual life. Some have tried other churches, and found that talking about spiritual life was not something with which people in the community were comfortable. Some congregations only allowed a very narrow spectrum of spiritual discussion to take place. Participants said that it was an incredible relief to be able, finally, to speak about spiritual things in a safe environment. They have found a place to be in touch with God's Spirit as it moves through the scripture, in the group sharing, and in the symbolic acts that are often part of the experience.

The sharing of spiritual experience is a profound gift we give one another. It is a way for God's Spirit to become enfleshed, embodied, real. It is a way for the Spirit to indeed dwell in our midst. It gives God space to *be* the encourager, the challenger, the confronter, the hoper, the healer, the life-transformer. But it is not only God's Spirit that gets space to breathe and *be* in such a place; those who share also come to see and know themselves as vehicles of the Spirit. This is an empowering, integrating, experience of being part of church community.

INTRODUCING IMAGERY TO THE GROUP

Participants need a sense of the overall structure of a session, so they know what to expect. This will help to create a sense of safe space. If people are new to meditation, or unfamiliar with it in the Christian tradition, I would use some of the material from An Ancient Art Made New, in Chapter 3. Some common concerns and questions are:

WHAT CAN I EXPECT?
Meditation needs practice. The first time, when one is on unfamiliar ground, meditators should be told not to set overly high expectations. Just relax and let be, and forget about achieving something.

WHAT IF I GO TO SLEEP?
Sometimes when a person becomes relaxed, as at the beginning of the meditation, sleep follows. This is because the body is used to sleeping when relaxation happens. Sleep can be a real gift of God. It may be exactly what is needed on a particular occasion, but it may mean that the person is resisting either the process of the meditation, or the particular content of the meditation. This may be a self-protection from dealing with material one is not yet ready for, or an opportunity for the depths of the soul to be reached in a more compassionate way. Each person needs to try to discern what is happening, and to decide what they want to do about it. It is possible to train the mind to stay awake during meditation, even though the body is in a state of complete relaxation. It is possible to develop an ability to be calm and to concentrate at the same time.

AM I BEING HYPNOTIZED OR CONTROLLED BY THE LEADER?

Meditators are always free in meditation. Each person is responsible for choosing how deeply they wish to enter a meditation. They are *not* being hypnotized or giving over control to you as leader. They can be aware at all times of what is happening and can choose to surface from the meditation whenever they wish, and to call in any extra help, such as Christ, or a person who is a mentor, or soul companion if they feel that would be helpful. This is particularly necessary for anyone who has experienced being under another's control. Since we have all been children, we all have some experience of this. This assurance of personal power is tremendously important if a person is to trust and let go in meditation.

SHOULD I MEDITATE IF I HAVE A HISTORY OF DISSOCIATION?

Those who have dissociative disorders should consult their therapists before doing meditation. For some it is healing. Others need to be more cautious. Each person is always in control of how deeply they will enter meditation.

WHAT IF MY MIND WANDERS?

It is not necessary to follow slavishly the suggestions of the leader. Perhaps a person's inner soul may need to focus in one place and stay with a particular part of the meditation. It may even suggest another direction. Each person's experience is unique, and it is not helpful to try to compare, or evaluate our experience, against those of others. Learning simply to trust and honour our own experience, learning to trust the God we encounter there, is already a great value.

There are distractions and mind-wandering chatter. Some will find it almost impossible to relax and to concentrate at the beginning. Unless we are used to practising silence, the mind quickly takes over its role of trying to help. It does this by reminding us of all the things we need to remember and by putting pictures and ideas into our mind. These distract us from being able to focus and centre.

When this happens, we can give ourselves negative messages about how poor we are at meditation, how impossible it is for us to concentrate or we can become very *earnest* about working hard to do meditation *right*.

Rather than putting a lot of energy into fighting mind-wandering mental chatter, it is better to befriend our mind. Trying too hard just creates tension that blocks effective meditation. We can thank our mind for trying to help us, but tell the mind that it can have a rest, because what we really need is to relax and practise the presence of God. It is amazing the effect that is created by this simple ritual of addressing our mind, almost as if it were a separate reality. We enlist its co-operation rather than waste energy fighting with it throughout the meditation.

Another approach is to accept the mind-wandering as a gift, as a reminder, as an indication of how much we need to meditate. Let the distraction pass gently out of awareness, rather than forcing it out by will. We might imagine these thoughts passing through our mind as clouds passing across the sky, or as leaves on a stream, gently allowing the wind or current to carry them away. Gently draw yourself back to the meditation, without moving into a self-judgemental mode.

What if I have Difficulty Visualizing?

There are different ways of experiencing visualization. Some see things quite clearly. For others, who find this more difficult, it is better not to try to see with the eyes, but rather to allow the visualization to come to the *mind's eye*. For some it may be more like the idea of an image or the sense or feeling of an image. It is important to refer to all the senses, and to all the ways of knowing — seeing, hearing, touching, smelling, feeling, thinking, intuiting. This honours our diversity in the ways we experience and know.

What if I Don't Remember What Happened?

Sometimes we may find we will not remember what happened in a meditation. This may mean we fell asleep, or it may mean that we were meditating very deeply and were not able to access it at that particular time. Meditations are somewhat like dreams. Some are vivid, and clearly meaningful; at other times we have a dream that is vague. Sometimes the images are simply confusing. It is important to remember that the process of meditating, in and of itself, has an effect even when we are not conscious of having received any particular insights. By developing our practice of meditating, we are telling our unconscious, as well as our conscious mind, that we value internal spiritual life and that we are prepared to invest in it. This has far-reaching results of which we are often not even aware. When we value the spiritual dimension, it opens an inner door that allows the Spirit more access to our consciousness. We give permission to the unconscious and to the wisdom stored there, to release its treasure trove of gifts.

THE ROLE OF THE LEADER

I hope that what I share here will not only give leaders confidence for leading these specific meditations, but also will be a stepping off point for developing other guided imagery meditations in the future. Anyone who leads meditation needs to be knowledgeable and well prepared. But, once these preparations are made, one of the most important gifts of a leader is a capacity for open listening to where the Spirit is leading the group. This involves letting go control. The leader's role is to provide a framework within which spiritual experience can happen. Leaders do not create the experience; what happens is an encounter between each meditator and the Spirit. This requires trust in the Spirit, for it requires the leader to wait upon, and to expect encounter with the Spirit in meditation. No one can make it happen, however. Leaders can create an open, trusting environment and, by preparing well, can lead meditations that will be helpful. But the real work of the session happens in the hearts, minds, and souls of all those who share the experience, quite beyond the control of the person leading.

Be prepared for the unexpected. God's Spirit blows where it chooses, and we do not always know where it comes from, or where it is going.[8] In my experience using meditation with groups, wisdom and truth have come often in the most unexpected places. Sometimes the most educated, successful participants have learned from people who have little or no status in the culture. Often the deepest experiences of God's presence come from the most vulnerable, the marginalized, the "least" in society's terms. They may have fewer barriers to hearing the good news, and have more "holes through which the holy can enter." Meditation creates a group where what normally gives power in the culture is not operative. It creates a radical equality that is a foretaste of God's reign.

Leading guided imagery meditation groups requires leaders who are attentive to the needs, vulnerabilities, and strengths of group members. The leader also needs to be attentive to his or her own spiritual journey, always on the lookout for what the Spirit is doing through the group. It is important to respect the diversity and the sacredness of each person coming to the group. Meditators need to find a safe place where they can share their experience with meditation. It has to be safe to share whatever happens, whether it is a spiritual awakening or an experience that might feel negative. Unless an atmosphere of trust is created in the group, participants will not feel free to "tell it like it is." They will only share the surface facts of their journey, and everyone will be impoverished. It is important for the leader to model the kind of trust and open sharing of experience. It is most useful to take the role of leader/participant as one who journeys alongside, rather than expert/teacher.

When you begin a meditation group, start with a contract for a set number of weeks. I would suggest four or six. This allows those who want to experiment to come to a group knowing that they will be free at the end of a set period to choose to come to another set of meditations, or to pursue other interests. We have worked with groups as large as twenty, but a group under fifteen is usually much better. For the sharing time following the meditation, sub-groups of six to ten are the best.

The Process
for Meditation Groups

B E F O R E   E A C H   S E S S I O N

a) The leader needs to be in touch with the scripture that is being meditated upon. She or he should have read it through several times, but also have allowed any images or feelings that emerge to resonate within.

b) It is important to think about and pray about the people who normally come to meditation.

c) Gather the materials needed for the group. I use
    - tape deck and music
    - cloth for a focal centre in the middle of the circle
    - candle (preferably the same one each week)
    - any symbols that connect with the images of the particular meditation. Suggestions are included with some of the meditations, but use your own creativity here. Sometimes a particular object seems to want to be in the centre even though you can not understand its particular connection. I have learned to trust these intuitive suggestions.
    - any additional materials to be used in the sharing (e.g. writing materials or clay).

d) Before each meditation, either at home before leaving, or before the group actually begins, do a silent invocation of the Healing Spirit of God, invoking the presence of Christ, or of Divine Light and Wisdom on the gathering. For me, this is an essential part of the preparation. It creates an attitude of responsiveness and openness that helps the leader "let go" of her or his own agenda and the need to control the outcome of the group.

As a leader, it is important to be attentive to the need for a balance between creating the safe *containing* space for the group, and creating the space for the "new thing God is doing in our midst." A very important way to do this is with a clear and simple process that is followed regularly, so that participants know what to expect. It is also important is to agree on clearly named group norms for the ways the group will function together. These simple structures give a sense of security, within which freedom can be experienced.

SETTING GROUP NORMS

At the first session group norms need to be established and clearly stated. Ones we have found important are:

a)   What happens inside the group is confidential, and is not to be shared outside the group.

b)   When a person shares a meditation, they are sharing holy ground and we need to listen to and honour that experience. Analyzing another person's meditation is almost never a good idea; it can make the person who is analyzed feel violated. As well, the interpretation usually says more about the interpreter and his or her particular issues, than it does about the meditator. However, the person who is sharing the meditation may choose to ask others for insights or associations. The leader needs to keep a very close eye on this particular dynamic, and it is best named as an issue in group norms, so that the whole group can be aware when this is happening, and take some responsibility for it.

c)   Participants are free to share at the level they feel comfortable, and to choose *not* to share.

SESSION OUTLINE

Our group has developed a very simple structure that is followed each week:
- Introduction
- Gathering
- Meditation
- Sharing
- Closure

INTRODUCTION

Each meditation has an introductory section that outlines the preparation needed for the session, the scriptures involved, and a reflection on the scriptures. You may want to share part or all of the reflection with the group, or you may find that this would be too directive. It is best not to read the scripture "cold," but rather to let the group warm up to being together first. You can also give the scripture reference(s) before the session so people have a chance to read them and think about them beforehand. This makes it easier to incorporate the scripture into your gathering activities. It is important to read the scripture aloud before the meditation, and to set it into any context that is needed.

GATHERING

Gathering is a time to check in with one another. It is important to go around the circle allowing everyone to introduce themselves (if there are those who do not know each other), and to speak *briefly* to a specific question or thought that is suggested. Although several ideas for gathering activities are suggested in each meditation, use only one or two per session. I always allow a time of silence after the introduction of an idea or question. This allows each person to go more deeply into themselves for a response that might not be available on the surface, and already begins the process of moving inside. This sharing process also begins the weaving together of the community.

Each meditation has some specific suggestions that I hope you will find appropriate to the particular theme. But each group is unique, and you may have other ideas that have worked for you in other situations. You may wish to choose from some of the ideas listed below:

a) As you come to meditation, be in touch with your deepest desire, your real yearning for this time. God often meets us in this place, the place where we are most longing. Indeed we might suggest that it is through these very yearnings that we are invited into relationship, into communion with the Spirit.
   - Where is this happening for you right now?
   - Where did you sense the Spirit's presence in the past week?

b) If you had to choose a colour to represent how you feel as you come to this group, what would that be?

c) Set the theme, then read the scripture and ask participants where they find themselves in it. Is there some word, or idea, or a particular person in the scripture that connects with you at this time in your life?

d)   Do a word association exercise around a text or an idea connected with the theme of the meditation.

e)   Play a piece of music and invite participants to share responses. If it has words, you may ask participants to share how they feel about a particular image of God that is referred to, and to suggest others that have power and meaning for them. You may also ask for a feeling response to the music. What feelings or associations are raised for you as you listened to the music?

MEDITATION

There are various phases of the actual meditation:
- Finding a comfortable position for your body-self.
- Preparing the spirit/body for meditation — putting the mind in a receptive, open, calm, clear state.
- Experiencing the imagery section of the meditation.
- Gradually drawing the group back to the circle and to their body-selves.
- Allowing silence for the experience to ground itself.

FINDING A COMFORTABLE POSITION

At this point, suggest that participants find a position where they can be comfortable. They may need to remove shoes or glasses, loosen a belt, or lie down. It is important in meditation for the spine to be in a straight line. Whether that happens by lying, or sitting on a chair, or sitting cross-legged on the floor is irrelevant. Let participants choose whichever is comfortable for them. Turn the lights down low, or even off if you are using a taped meditation and do not need to read it. (Check with the group if there are any members for whom darkness is a problem.) Put the tape player on if you are using music behind your own reading. There is a lot of meditative music available on the market these days, but much of it has too much tune or melody. The more amorphous, repetitive, and non-distracting the sound, the better. It needs to be like waves on which one can rest and be supported, but beware of using actual water sounds as it stimulates the reflex to urinate.

If you are not using taped meditations, but are leading with your own voice, it is important to pace the meditation well. Leave long silences and pauses regularly in the meditation. If you are a beginner, practise leaving pauses that seem overly long to you, since your own perception of the passing of time is usually an underestimate of the length of silence needed for those you are guiding. Your voice needs to be gentle and flowing, coming from a deep place inside you. You need to do the body relaxation part of the meditation yourself so that your voice is coming from

[27]

your centre. If you are leading meditation with a large group, use a microphone rather than projecting your voice stridently.

At the end of your sessions ask for feedback from those you are guiding, so you will know the speed and volume that is appropriate for the group you are leading.

PREPARING THE SPIRIT/BODY FOR MEDITATION

"Stilling" or "mindfulness" is the first step in meditating, before one begins the more active part of the meditation of looking for insight or depth understanding of the images. Chilean psychiatrist Claudio Naranjo distinguishes between the *mindfulness* and the *God-mindfulness* stages of meditation. At the *mindfulness* stage one is gaining awareness of the immediate sensations in one's body, the emotions one is feeling, or the thoughts that arise and pass away. At the *God-mindfulness* stage, the meditator gains wisdom and insight by focusing on an external symbol or image.[9]

It is important not to move too quickly through this stage of stilling the body because it is an essential foundation for the quality of the imaging to follow. The amount of time required for this depends upon the stress the participants bring to the time of meditation and their experience of meditation. With experience, one can learn to move into meditative state much more quickly. It is as if the brain has learned new patterns that affect the body's ability to relax and let go. For many, the paying attention to the body/spirit-self is, in itself, an important source of insight, as the meditator begins to listen, and pay attention to the wisdom of the body, to the wisdom of feelings, and to inner thought patterns.

EXPERIENCING THE IMAGERY SECTION OF THE MEDITATION

Since each individual meditation in the resource deals specifically with this aspect of the meditation, I will make only some general comments here. Please note that there is some repetition from meditation to meditation in the relaxation/preparation section. Familiar words in this section help participants to unwind and find a safe place from which to embark. Any repetition is, therefore, intentional and is reprinted on each meditation in order to eliminate flipping back and forth in the book during the meditation section of the session.

After the relaxation/preparation section, I normally begin by grounding the meditators in a place that is safe for them. Sometimes I will suggest a safe place that is connected with the meditation. Sometimes, they are simply invited to imagine themselves in a place that is safe and comfortable for them. This may be a place they know, or it may be a place they create in their imagination. If there are very deeply wounded people in your group, don't be surprised if they have a lot of difficulty with this. Tragically, there are people who have never in all their lives experienced a place where they felt safe. Gently remind participants that they can create one for themselves, and then return to it whenever they choose.

To be really grounded, imaginatively means using all the senses — getting a sense of the colours, of the smells, of the sounds, of the textures, of the feeling of sun or breeze on the skin.

At the end of the meditation it is important to return to the same place from which one began, and to be there for a few seconds before being gradually and gently brought back to the group, back to awareness of their breath, and body-self.

At the end of a meditation, a period of silence is needed to ground the meditation, to let it take root in consciousness. Some will want to journal or draw at this time. It is a time to move from what happened inside, during meditation, to prepare to share the experience with others. This takes a few moments.

LANGUAGE FOR THE HOLY PRESENCE

For leading meditations, I have found Carolyn Stahl's advice on language about God and Christ to be very helpful.[10] The more open the symbol, the more it evokes. When I am doing a meditation specifically around the historical Jesus, I may refer to "Jesus," but often I find that the term "the Christ" evokes something broader than the historical person. In our group experience "Christ" has come in images both male and female, as a child, as healing light, as living water, as a gardener, as a vine, as a particular person in whom a meditator has experienced Christ-presence, or as an awareness of presence, of power, of energy, but not necessarily as an image. By being too concrete in imaging the Holy, we can block God's Spirit from manifesting itself in the way the Spirit desires. We can lock God or Christ imagery into such tight boxes, that God doesn't get a chance to come to us in the way God wants, or in the way we are able to receive.

I never cease to be amazed by the versatility and ingenuity of the Spirit in the ways it breaks through to various individuals. And it never ceases to move me how totally appropriate the particular image is for the meditator. As pastor, I am often privy to deep personal issues in the lives of those in the group. It is nothing short of miraculous to watch the God who finds exactly the right way to reach each person.

I have found that the word "God" sometimes carries a lot of baggage in people's histories and unfortunately often evokes an image of a rigid, judgemental, uncaring presence. There are others who need to hear the more traditional language in order to feel safe in meditation.

When I have a lot of people in recovery in the group, I use the term "Higher Power" several times, so that they can connect that familiar concept to the Holy of which I am speaking. I think most of us in the church would do well to reflect on Moses' encounter with the burning bush where *The Name* was given. It is an almost untranslatable *I Am who I Am, I will be who I will be, I am Being-ness Becoming*; not exactly a concrete image one can "nail down." Yet even this ineffable name was considered to be so sacred that it could not be spoken. Other words that stood for the unspeakable *Name* were used (e.g. words that have been translated as "Lord").

Jesus, in trying to show that this Holy Reality was not only other-ness and far away, used the term *abba*. This was shocking at the time, because it was an intimate term of family endearment "dadda." Jesus knew that God was more than the images that had been used up to that time.

I use God imagery that is as open and as symbolic as possible. I also use a wide variety of words. In this way I hope I am letting God fill in the spaces. The Holy Presence comes with freedom in the way it desires and chooses.

LETTING FLOW

It is important to *let be* in meditation. Do not try to force images, or use meditation as a means to an end. Meditation itself is worthwhile, whether it yields any deep wisdom or not. Expectations of how or what one *should* see only block the process. Just concentrate on the visual journey and let it take you where it will. Do not censor images that you cannot understand or that do not seem "holy." What is needed is an attitude of waiting upon the presence of the Spirit.

In the meditation, often I will suggest that the person bring a gift to the Holy Presence (allowing space for that to emerge as it will), and that they receive a gift from the Sacred One. This is a way of grounding the meditation, and bridging the inner experience of the visualization and the conscious everyday reality of one's life.

MAKING SENSE OF IMAGES AND SYMBOLS

Certain images have fairly widespread symbolic meaning. In most bookstores and libraries there are dictionaries of symbols for looking up images.[11] The following are fairly widely accepted interpretations:

- **Water imagery** usually is connected with the unconscious. If it is a river, it may connect with the flow of one's life and the flow of energy or of feelings.
- **Butterflies** often symbolize transformation, resurrection.
- **Houses or buildings** usually have something to do with the self and with how one experiences the self. The basement moves deeper into the unconscious, the rooftop the connection with the divine.

- **Paths and roads** usually connect with one's life course, and have something to say about how we are experiencing that journey.
- **Seeds, plants, trees**, have to do with growth, or some aspect of growth.
- **A baby** often means a new thing that is being born in one's life, a part of you that is still new and vulnerable, but which has great potential for growth.
- **A wise person** often means wisdom or inner guidance. Sometimes they are the mediator between God and the self.
- **The moon** usually represents female sacred energy and the tugging power that creates ebb and flow. It may represent a gentle, wisdom-light in the darkness.
- **The sun** may represent male sacred energy, energy for action, for growth, for warmth.

While these are some fairly widespread understandings of symbols, when a symbol emerges it does so in the particular context of a person's life and so the same symbol may have different meanings for different people. It is important not to be too rigid with interpretation.

Images may relate to various levels of meaning both in dreams, and in meditation. The image may be about something directly connected with one's external world. Or it may connect with inner reality and with the processes, emotional and spiritual, that are happening within. Sometimes the images work on a variety of levels at once. The experience of running up against an invisible wall of resistance on a journey may refer to some roadblock in the outer world. It may connect with inner barriers, or it may symbolize resistance that must be faced and named.

What happens in meditation may be very subtle — nothing nameable, not an image, not a phrase, not a feeling even — but a profound knowing that is transformative. The meditator enters a process of the death of the ego, so that the higher self, the God-self can become more rooted in the meditator. In the losing, in the letting go, one finds a treasure of great price, a more complete self, more compassionate, connected, differentiated, joy-filled, courageous, grounded, passionate, creative, free. These qualities will be recognized as ones very present in Jesus.

It is this process of transformation that I believe scripture is talking about when it speaks of losing the self but gaining the whole world. It is what mystics have spoken of for centuries; this vast expansion of being that happens when the small-self is released. Jesus spoke of being born again and of entering the reign of God. But this often happens in subtle ways, like the planting of a mustard seed or the tiny, unseen yeast in the dough.

Meditations are not something used once then thrown aside. The same meditation can be done over and over again. Each time the meditator is a different person experiencing the meditation; so there is always the possibility of a "new thing" arising. As well, when you find a particular meditation that speaks deeply to you, it is good to go into it again; perhaps to place yourself in the scene in a different way in order to experience more levels of the meditation. Feeling, listening, observing what is happening in the meditation, and noticing how it is affecting you is a process that can be repeated over and over, with new insights gained.

I have a particular meditation, The Healing Pool, that speaks deeply to me. Whenever I begin meditation and go to a safe place, this is most often where I will go. After years with this image, I find I can enter it quite quickly and go to the familiar place and a sense of calm, of inner peace, of well-being comes over me almost immediately when I picture it in my mind's eye. It keeps unfolding new truth and insight, and in this place I meet the Holy often.

SILENCE FOR GROUNDING THE MEDITATION
At the end of meditation, it is good to leave a period of silence, with the music playing, before beginning to speak. This is an important transition time between the inner experience and sharing that experience with others.

SHARING
The sharing segment of each meditation includes two basic sections: silence for journalling and debriefing. Some specific suggestions appear with the meditations but it is important to keep these general suggestions in mind for each session.

Some participants find it helpful to ground their experience by journalling. Give space to those who wish to write down or draw their insights. Ask them to note any particular image, word, phrase, feeling, understanding that came to them. Encourage each person to ask themselves the question, "What does this experience mean for my life?" They may or may not share this writing with others.

After silence and journalling, invite the participants to share what they wish from their meditation. Allow participants to share as they feel moved, rather than going around the circle. Groups of seven or under are best for sharing meditation experiences. When we have had large groups, we have divided into smaller groups for sharing.

Sharing the experience soon after having it helps to ground the experience in consciousness and to listen for its meaning. I have often said in our groups that by sharing and honouring our spiritual experience we resist the culture's devaluation of the spiritual, of intuition, of imagination, of feeling, and of experience. To have one's sacred experience witnessed helps the meditator to integrate it more fully.

For those who have the privilege of listening, it can also bring spiritual wealth and wisdom. Sharing of spiritual experience is one of the greatest gifts we can offer to one another.

As a leader, at this stage of the session, I am listening particularly for what God has been doing in the meditation. I try to lift up the meditator's own experience of God for the person to see and to savour, so that it can take root more deeply. We have one group member who is quite shy. When the Spirit gives him a particular insight it is usually in the form of a message or a gift, but he has a tendency to skip over it very quickly when he talks about it. I repeat back the words that he has been given, mirror them back to him, and help him to integrate the gift. In this way I help him to receive and reinforce the power of his experience. This is the type of response that is most useful in sharing, rather than moving into analyzing and intellectualizing.

When just out of a meditation, meditators are very vulnerable and open. They have lowered their barriers. Their holy ground must be approached with great respect, "with our shoes removed" so to speak. A good rule is that we are to hear one another's experience, to witness it, to receive it as a sacred gift. Our role is to help each other savour and honour the experience. We are not there to analyze, to problem solve, or to fix one another. Without this fundamental attitude, an atmosphere of safety is not created.

A meditation is not good or bad in itself. Its meaning cannot be abstracted from the context in which it was experienced, which is the life-journey of the meditator. Therefore it is very dangerous, and presumptuous, for others to assume that they are better placed to understand the meaning of a meditation than the meditator her- or himself.

As with dreams, beware the interpretations of others, beware allegorical explanations, beware literal interpretations. Most problems and tensions have arisen in our group when one group member tried to interpret another's meditation through their own filters. This can have the effect of stealing the experience from the one who had it; or of putting the experience into an inappropriate box.

It can be helpful for others to suggest what the story evokes for them. This gives the fellow meditator the opportunity to connect with each insight or not, as they feel appropriate. Questions to help clarify or to open up the telling of the story can also be helpful, as long as they do not probe too much. Permission needs to be explicitly given so that the person sharing their experience can ask the questioner to stop at any time. The leader needs to be the gatekeeper, especially if the person sharing the meditation is not very assertive.

Those with the most positive experiences will usually share first. Someone who feels that their experience is negative, or that "nothing has happened" often holds back, unsure if it is safe to share. The first person who shares such an experience gives the group a great gift because it creates safety for others to be completely real with their own experience.

Meditation is not a failure if you do not hear bells ringing and have no Technicolour movies rolling. When someone tells me that "nothing happened," I ask them to tell me about that "nothing." Often in what one thought was "nothing," there can be insight about what was blocking or what was causing resistance. Sometimes the "nothing" holds feelings of alienation or fear of feeling. This, in itself, can be the spiritual insight the Spirit is offering. Accepting what is, trying to discern the meaning of all experience, is a necessary attitude. There are no fixed rules around experience that participants are supposed to *obey*.

We need to cultivate wisdom and grounded-ness in reflecting on the meditations in order to distinguish truth from illusion. We need to be able to distinguish the results of mind-chatter from deep spiritual wisdom, and to practise reliable thinking about meditation. Reality in meditations does not obey the same rules as reality in daily life. It has more of a dream-reality quality — very profound in its power to heal, give wisdom, and even insight and direction to one's life, but not to be taken literally and acted on in a literal fashion. We know that some dreams have great power, wisdom, and truth; while some are just the unconscious processing of the last night's movie or some experience you have just had. Discernment of meaning is important.

The most negative experiences in groups I have been associated with have been with the very few people who felt that they needed to *produce*, week after week, cosmic transformative meditations. This kind of spiritual grandstanding shows real insecurity. The participant's actual experience is not felt to be adequate so they manufacture an experience in order to have status in the group. The tragedy is that, until this attitude changes, a spiritual lie is created and that insulates the meditator from the genuine experience they so deeply desire.

It is important for a leader to be able to confront this gently if it is happening. I have done this by talking about how we know when something is a "real" experience and when it is just from our mind-chatter, conscious, ego part of our psyche. The participants can inevitably come up with a list that helps us all become more conscious and more critical (in a good sense) of the experiences we hear. It is easy to recognize the difference in quality and in feeling between genuine experience and encounter and experience that is generated out of ego needs.

Genuine experience has a palpable feeling of integrity. It comes with surprise, usually, because it is not what the meditator expected. It is rooted in relationship with God, and is not just talking about what the person thinks God might feel or think. It has a transformational quality to it that speaks to the soul of the person. The listener senses that it comes from the very core, and so it has authority. Often tears accompany it, or some other emotional reaction. It is also congruent with the experience of God that we know through Christ.

It is important that times of spiritual dryness be acknowledged, and even honoured, as an important part of the spiritual journey. There are desert periods on the spiritual journey. We might feel God is completely absent and that our lives are just going in circles. We might not even be able to see where God is providing manna and water because this nurture comes in unfamiliar places. Experiences that are interpreted as negative need to be talked about and examined. This creates trust in a group and the permission to be real. This is vital for the healthy life of the group.

If a person has not shared at the end of the group, I ask if there is anyone else who would like to share before we draw the group to an end. In this way there is no pressure to share, but no one is cut off by unexpected closure.

Sometimes it is helpful to share the meditation with a trusted friend or spiritual guide, a minister or spiritual director, as well as sharing with the group. I am sometimes concerned about those who do not share with anyone in order to help them process the experience. The leader needs to be available after the group for at least one half-hour in case there is someone who needs to talk privately, or there are those who want to make appointments for another time. Often this will not be necessary, but it is good to be aware that it may be needed.

CLOSURE

This is usually a very brief part of the session. Often I will ask each person to reflect on how they saw God "being" for them in their meditation, and to call out the one or two words that best describe this. It is amazing to hear words like comforting, challenging, showing, encouraging, clarifying, reminding, healing, unsettling, disturbing, being absent, stirring up, inviting, connecting, and so many more. We know we have experienced a Presence that is active and alive in our times and in our lives.

At other times I ask participants to look around the circle to see the face of God in each one present, and to offer blessing and peace to one another. I invite participants to remember these faces during the week, and the stories they have shared in this gathering, and to hold one another in the Spirit in the following week.

A closure may include a particular ritual e.g. using water, or salt, or light, or the sharing of seeds or stones. Where something specific seems appropriate, I have suggested it in the meditation itself. These three general closing rituals are appropriate for many meditations.

1. A Body Blessing

Stand in a circle. Explain the movements slowly and prayerfully. I have found that it works best if only the person leading has the words. This helps those praying to focus on praying the body itself, rather than on trying to read words. You may wish to have copies available for participants to take home so that they can integrate this prayer into their personal prayer time.

When there are persons with physical disabilities in the group, it is important to be sensitive to their needs. In such circumstances, the blessing might be introduced with an acknowledgement that it is a group with differing physical abilities, but we can celebrate and bless the bodies we have. Where a person is not able to do the actions, you could suggest that they do what they can and allow their imagination to help with the rest of the action.

Honouring that which is most Holy,
> *(Hands together in prayer mode in front of the heart.)*

Accept from me,
> *(Gradually open hands and raise arms above head in prayer gesture.)*

The Spirit of my Soul.
> *(Bring hands facing forward together over head so that the little fingers link together. This forms a kind of butterfly or spirit symbol. Draw this "butterfly" down to the heart as you say "soul.")*

I place it in this vessel,
> *(Hands come down to abdominal level and form a cup container. Feel the weight of the offering it contains.)*

And offer it up.
> *(Raise the hand container slowly and intentionally above the head as an offering to God.)*

Pour down your gentle blessing upon me,
> *(Open hands, turn palms towards you as you move fingers in a rain-like movement down to your shoulders.)*

As I stand before you with an open heart.
> *(Open hands, palms forward, moved to sides at shoulder level, in an attitude of surrender and openness.)*

Bless my mind that it may think with clarity and wisdom.
> *(Hands touch the head.)*

Bless my eyes that they may see beauty and truth around me.
> *(Touch eyes.)*

Bless my ears that they may hear the pain and joy of life.
> *(Touch ears.)*

Bless my mouth that I may speak your truth.
> *(Touch mouth.)*

Bless my heart that I may have the passion and compassion to respond.
> *(Touch heart.)*

Bless my whole body that it may be a temple of your Spirit.
> *(One hand on heart, another on abdomen.)*

Bless my hands that they may touch life with tenderness and healing.
> *(Open hands.)*

Bless my feet that they may root me to the earth and carry me
> where you would have me go.
> *(Reach out towards feet, not necessarily touching them.)*

Bless my soul that it may always join me to your Love and to the world
> You created and love.
> *(Raise hands in a straight line through the centre of the body above the head, then open them outwards to make a circle as you say the words. At the end reach out to take the hand of the person on either side of you as you are ending this line.)*

2. EXCHANGE OF PEACE

We often close by offering peace to one another. It is important to remind the group that there are those who need and love hugs, and there are those who are not at all comfortable with them. We always need to ask permission to hug. Many women who have been abused by men, and who have come to the group unable to stand any physical contact with a man, have met loving, caring, nurturing, vulnerable men in our groups and have been able to receive and to ask for hugs for the first time in their lives. The freedom to refuse to be touched is part of what helps to make acceptance on a future occasion possible. It is also important to remind the group that while some believe a firm handshake is a sign of character, others with arthritis, osteoporosis, etc. cannot stand the pressure of a firm handshake.

3. CLOSURE SONG

Sometimes it is appropriate to sing a closure. This depends upon your group's size and comfort with singing. It also depends upon the mood of the group at the end of the gathering. There are many songs that are useful for closure. Some specific

suggestions are made with individual mediations. Here are some general suggestions from *Voices United*. The complete song index is on page 200.

- Spirit of Life
- Breathe on Me, Breath of God
- The Lone, Wild Bird (selected verses)
- Spirit of the Living God
- Come and Find the Quiet Centre
- Amazing Grace
- God is Passionate Life (adding healing or other appropriate words)
- Go Now in Peace
- May the blessing of God go before you
- The Lord bless thee, and keep thee
- Stay with Us through the night

PART II

Meditations for Healing and Forgiveness

MEDITATION

1

THE TEMPLE OF THE SPIRIT
THE MIND-BODY-SPIRIT CONNECTION

INTRODUCTION

PREPARATION

- paper and pens/pencils/drawing materials
- candle
- open Bible
- some pictures that would evoke places one would consider sacred/temples
- a picture of one or more people

SCRIPTURE: 1 CORINTHIANS 3:16

You may wish to refer to the earlier section of the letter (2:10–15), where Paul speaks of the Spirit searching a person and revealing wisdom and truth and an ability to discern the value of everything.

REFLECTION

This meditation is a fairly simple opening of the body and mind to experience the Spirit of God that dwells within. Many of us have grown up with poor body image; some even with body hatred integrated into the unconscious mind. Whether we realize it or not, this attitude and message permeates every cell of our body, as well as our emotional, and spiritual life. Low self-esteem, de-energizing depression, and even physical illness can result.

Experiencing oneself as the temple in which the Spirit dwells can be profoundly powerful for someone who needs healing from self-hatred. Some participants will discover surprising resistance to this experience of being the dwelling place of the Holy. That knowledge can be a powerful insight, for it reveals to a person how deeply ingrained those negative images and attitudes are.

This meditation is useful for those experiencing chronic pain or physical or emotional illness. It is helpful for those who have experienced abuse and feel that their bodies are shameful. It helps to ground the person who does the meditation in the grace and Spirit of God, which is healing and integrating.

In a shortened form, it could be used at the beginning of any of the meditations as a relaxation, grounding exercise. (Also, refer to the introduction to the meditation Created in God's Image, page 46.)

GATHERING

a) Notice your body. Are you aware of any places in your body where you are storing tension, stress, fear, anger, anxiety, other emotions?

b) Give your body a name, and describe it as if it were another person.
    - What age is it?
    - What does it think and feel?
    - How would it describe itself to you and to others?

c) Where have you learned the messages you hear in your head about your body? What are they?

d) See also Gathering Activities from Created in God's Image.

MEDITATION

Shut your eyes ... let yourself begin to connect with this body-self that you are ... this holy temple ... Many of us spend our whole lives disconnected from our body-self ... We take our body for granted ... We do not recognize it as created in God's image ... as a source of wisdom and profound knowing ... Ask your body to teach you its wisdom as your relax ... as you tell your mind that it does not need to help you for the next while ... that it is good for you to relax and just be for the next little while ... Tell your mind that it can take a rest ... that you appreciate that it is trying to help, but that just for now you want to be fully present to your body-self ... and to its wisdom ...

	TICKET NUMBER
	SCHEDULED DATE
	ROUTE / SEQUENCE

568668

08/21/02

743 000 /60

604-988-9398   2-BD

MAP:

ES	AVERAGE	ORDERED	PRODUCT CODE	DELIVERED	RETURNED
3 2	2.6	2	10005	2	2

ROW HOW MUCH IN A LIFETIME?

ORDER DATE	CASH RECEIVED	CUSTOMER SIGNATURE
8/20/02		

COPY

CANADIANSPRINGS
WATER-COMPANY

DEL

Vancouver	Victoria
604 232-7600	250 727-9100

TOLL FREE
GS

WE DELIVER *Pure* SATISFACTION

```
WICHROWSKE, MARGARET
UNIT 302
555 28 ST. W
NORTH VANCOUVER BC V7N2J7

:TKT TO DEL 2 BTLS AUG 21
```

PRODUCT DESCRIPTION		PREVIOU
PREMIUM WATER — 18 L	807	
	723	

```
Q:THE AVERAGE PERSONS HAIR W
A: 590 INCHES
```

ACCOUNT NUMBER	NEXT DELIVERY	SALES F
01-347360	09/05/2002	LKWA

CUST

As you begin to pay attention to your body, do you notice places where tension is stored up? ... where your muscles are in tight knots? ... As you scan your body, from the top of your head to the bottom of your feet ... notice if there are tender places ... sore spots ... and send compassion to these places in your body, thanking them for the hard work they are doing ... perhaps offering to pay more attention to what they are telling you in the future ... Befriend the places of pain in your body...

Become aware of your breathing ... of the life-sustaining breath that goes on all of the time ... even when you are unaware ... Notice if you are breathing with only a small part of your lungs, or whether you are taking the breath deeply into your whole being ... down to the bottom of your lungs ... Breathe with your whole torso ... your whole body... Take the breath of life up to the tops of your shoulders ... a place where many of us store stress and the heavy loads we are carrying ... Take your breath down to the bottom of your lungs, down near your waist ... Notice if your tummy moves in and out as you inhale and exhale ... the way a baby's does when it is breathing naturally ...

Notice where you are tightened up ... not fully open to the breath of life ... Let your body relax ... let the tension flow out of your body through your feet ... Begin to allow your breath to move deeper into your being ... taking the breath deep down into your belly... creating inner space ...

Breathe in deeply the healing presence of the Spirit ... the goodness and grace of God ... Take it right into your centre ... With each breath out, allow the breath to carry away the toxins that have built up ... the physical poisons that need to be cleansed ... Let it also carry out the emotional poisons that have been stored in your body ... the pains and angers that need to be let go ...

Let the healing breath gently caress the wounded places ... let the life-giving breath of God work in a healing, cleansing way in your body-self ... in your emotional-self ... in your spirit-self ... Let the rhythm of taking in newness and healing ... and letting go of built-up tensions and stress ... take root in this time of meditation ... Know that this is a force for deep inner healing that is planted in you by the Creator ... and that this is a power you may access whenever you want, or need to ... The breath keeps your body open ... allowing it to do its work ... allowing the energies to flow ...

Breathe in possibility ... Breathe in the hope that the Spirit gives ... Let go of the stress and tensions that are stored in your body-self ... your emotional-self ... your spiritual-self ... Breathe in life energy ... The creating breath of God that was there from the beginning ... Breathe out whatever would block you from being fully present to this time ... Again notice your body ... If there continue to be tense places, imagine the healing breath moving directly to those spots ... unknotting the tension ... letting go ... letting be ... letting open ... letting unlock ...

As you give yourself the gift of relaxation, the gift of embodiment ... notice the inner space created by this letting go ... Notice how much this tension that has built up in you had been blocking your inner life ... your core-self ... how much it has been keeping you from being in touch with your sacred centre ... As your prepare this space, know that there is nowhere more important to be ... that there is nothing more important to do ... than to be present ... to yourself ... to the Holy Presence ... to the Spirit ... to your deep silent centre ...

Imagine your body-self as a sacred holy place ... a temple of the Spirit ... a place that deserves to be cared for and honoured ... Allow yourself to open to the presence of the Spirit that dwells within you ... that lives through you ... The very presence and power and spirit of God lives in you ... Let yourself feel the sacred energy and power of the Spirit in you ... Let yourself feel the healing energy and power of the Spirit in you ... Let yourself feel the comforting energy and power of the Spirit in you ... Let yourself feel the strengthening power of the Spirit in you ... Let yourself feel the loving power of the Spirit in you ... Let yourself feel the creating power of the Spirit in you ... Let yourself feel the challenging power of the Spirit in you ...

What wisdom would the Spirit want to offer you right now? ... What truth would the Spirit want you to know? ... What gift would the Spirit want you to receive?

Gradually become aware of your body as you are sitting (or lying) ... Notice your breathing ... Make some gentle movements with your fingers ... your toes ... your neck and shoulders ... When you are ready, gradually open your eyes.

SHARING

JOURNALLING/DRAWING

DEBRIEFING

Ask everyone to share, as they feel comfortable, what happened for them in the meditation:

· What was it like for you to feel yourself relax?
· Could you experience the power of the breath as healing?
· What happened when you began to imagine your body as a temple of the Spirit?

CLOSURE

a) There is a Christian tradition of breath prayer, which uses the rhythm of the breath to create a mantra-like prayer. Each person could be invited to find their own breath prayer to create affirmation. Invite participants to pray in this way daily and keep repeating their prayer until it becomes part of them. Examples are:

"Be still and know" (on the breath in)
"that I am God"(on the breath out).

"I am worthy" (on the breath in)
"I release fear" (on the breath out)

"I am healing" (on the breath in)
"I rest in God" (on the breath out)

b) The Body Blessing, in Chapter 5, would work especially well with this meditation.

MEDITATION

2

---❖---

CREATED IN GOD'S IMAGE

INTRODUCTION

PREPARATION
- paper and pens/pencils/drawing materials
- mirror

SCRIPTURE: GENESIS 1:1–2
Psalm 139:1–18, 23 or John 1:1–14 would also work well for this meditation.

REFLECTION

Our bodies are often experienced as alien, as problems, as obstacles that must be overcome, or instruments to be used in our quest for living the "real" life that comes from our rational, thinking minds. Many of us have spent our whole lives finding something wrong with our bodies. Many of us grew up actually despising the way we look.

In the culture, there are all kinds of invitations to despise the body and to blame it for our lack of happiness, or fulfilment. We are invited to try this miracle diet, or buy that particular brand of toiletry to hide the natural body "stench." We need to dress in particular ways in order to be accepted. We need to dye our hair, or implant hair if we are balding. When we become ill or tired, we treat our bodies as if they are letting us down, rather than having compassion for them for being used in abusive overwork.

We ignore our bodies when they are not in pain. We dislike them for not fitting the image created for them. We dislike them for the natural processes of ageing. We punish them for the messages of pain that would invite our attentiveness, or for the messages of fatigue that would slow our driven path. As we age, we are brainwashed into seeing the changes in our body as a scandal, an enemy that must be contended with, controlled, fought against.

Yet our bodies are like photographic films on which are imprinted the memories of unhealed hurts of our bodily and emotional experience. We are not disembodied minds or spirits. Our bodies ARE ourselves. They are a source of wisdom and knowing. They offer truth that we can not know in other ways. They are the avenue through which we encounter and interface with the rest of creation.

In the Hebraic tradition the word *nephesh* was used for body/spirit. There was no separation. In Christian tradition we speak of incarnation. We speak of the Word becoming flesh and dwelling among us full of grace and truth.[12] In Genesis 1, God speaks of creation as "good." What would it mean for us actually to experience our body-selves being blessed by the Creating God as "good"? For many of us, this would be a radical conversion of our thinking and being.

This particular meditation came from working with women who had internalized self-hatred. Marie-Thérèse Porcile, a Uruguayan theologian, spoke of doing something similar with the women she worked with in the slums of her country. The notion of being created in God's image was for them, as for the women with whom I was working, an impossible concept. At some level, for all of these women, their image of God was still male. They could not imagine themselves created in God's image. They were bearing in their bodies and spirits, often unconsciously, the wounds of sexism, denigration of women, and body-hatred. Many had been sexually or physically violated as children or adults. These wounds were sapping their self-esteem, destroying hope, and leading to despair and powerlessness.

I began to do this meditation with women both in the group, but also in individual sessions. For many, it was very healing. Some have told me that they have done this as a regular prayer meditation and it has very powerfully affected their feelings of self-worth and self-acceptance over a period of time. One woman said that it was the first time she had ever been able to get a sense of God actually loving her, rather than judging her as inadequate.

As this meditation was sometimes done in a mixed group, it was also fascinating for men to hear women's experiences, and to come into touch with their own alienation from their body-selves. For many of the men, it became an important meditation for integrating body and spirit, and for healing their own embodied memories.

GATHERING

a)   Notice your body. Become aware of where you are storing tension and stress, or locking up anger, fear or pain. Is there any wisdom there for you? What is giving you a pain in the neck? What is stabbing you between the shoulder blades? What is tying your guts in knots? What is hard to swallow, that is making your throat tense? What are you gritting your teeth and locking your jaw to keep from letting out? (other examples?)

b)   If you were asked to stand in front of a mirror and look at your full body-self, would you find that difficult or easy? How would you feel about what you saw?

c)   Where have you received the messages that have affected how you feel about your body? As you reflect back over your childhood and youth, then into adulthood, what are some of the factors that have created your attitudes?

MEDITATION

Close your eyes ... Let yourself pay attention to what it feels like to be in this body-self that is you today ... right now ... Most of us go through whole days ... sometimes our whole lives ... without really paying attention to this body-self ... In Hebrew, the language Jesus knew, there was no such thing as disembodied spirit ... They spoke of the *nephesh* ... the body-soul ... the spirit/body ... Jesus talked about our bodies as temples of the Spirit ... What is it like for you to think of yourself in that way?

As you begin to pay attention to your body, do you notice places where tension is stored up? ... where your muscles are in tight knots? ... As you scan your body, from the top of your head to the bottom of your feet ... notice if there are tender places ... sore spots ... and send compassion to these places in your body, thanking them for the hard work they are doing ... perhaps offering to pay more attention to what they are telling you in the future ... Become aware of your breathing, this life-sustaining process that goes on all of the time, even when we are unaware ... Notice if you are breathing with only a small part of your lungs, or whether you are taking the breath deeply into your whole being, down to the bottom of your lungs

... up to the tops of your shoulders ... Notice if your tummy moves in and out as you inhale and exhale ... the way a baby's does when it is breathing naturally ...

Notice where you are tightened up ... not fully open to the breath of life ... Let your body relax ... let the tension flow out of your body through your feet ... Begin to allow your breath to move deeper into your being ... taking the breath deep down into your belly ... creating inner space ... Breathe in deeply the healing presence of the Spirit ... the goodness and grace of God ... Take it right into the core of your being ... As you breathe out, let the breath carry with it the poisons ... physical ... emotional ... spiritual ... that have built up in your system ... Breathe in possibility ... hope that the Spirit gives ... Let go of the stress and tensions that are stored in your body-self ... your emotional-self ... your spiritual-self ... Breathe in life energy ... The creating breath of God that was there from the beginning ... Breathe out whatever would block you from being fully present to this time...

Again notice your body ... If there continue to be tense places, imagine this healing breath moving directly to those spots ... unknotting the tension ... letting go ... letting be ... letting open ... letting unlock ... Know that you are in a safe place ... that this is a place where it is safe to be ... Notice the inner space that is being prepared and opened up inside you ... space for the Sacred Presence to find room ... Space for the Holy One to be with you ... Your own sacred space ... your own holy ground ... Your own sacred centre ...

In Genesis the Spirit breathes over the waters and there is life ... God speaks and there is life ... the word of God ... the breath of Spirit ... the wisdom of God ... creating ... making life out of chaos ... order out of disorder ... Get some sense or feeling of this creating living force ... In your imagination allow this living Spirit to create you ...

Experience the Spirit creating your feet ... Knitting together all of the bones that make up your feet ...Creating the strong bones that will be needed to support all your weight ... Imagine the Spirit adding all of the small bones and tendons that allow for flexibility ... Get a sense of all of the muscles that connect these bones ... Sense the creation of the toes with their intricate flexibility ... Feel the blood vessels that bring food to the cells of your feet ... and to the nerve endings that feel the earth ... that help you sense your balance ... God looks at the incredible miracle of your feet and says ... It is good. It is good ...

Next imagine the Spirit creating your legs ... placing just so ... the strong bones that will have to carry so much weight ... Creating flexibility for movement with the complex structure that is your knee ... Become aware of the bone ... the cartilage ... the tendons and sinews that hold it together ... Get a sense of the complex muscle structure in your legs ... connecting to the rest of your body for strength ... for movement ... this structure that allows you to walk ... to run ... to bend ... to lift ... to play ... to work ... Become aware of the artery and vein system that carries blood ... bringing life-giving oxygen to your body ... the circulatory system that carries away wastes that have built up in your tissues ... Become aware of the nerves that go through your legs to pass messages from your brain ... Notice the skin covering ... all that the Spirit has created ... this miracle of your legs ... and God looks with great delight on this part of God's creation and says It is good ... It is very good ...

Then experience the Spirit creating your hips for strength and movement ... a cradle for your internal organs ... Imagine the Spirit creating your genitals ... and your reproductive system ... with its amazing capacity to give and to receive pleasure ... with its capacity to create and nurture life ... Imagine the Spirit creating the intricacy of your digestive system ... Imagine the Spirit creating the complexity of all of the glands ... Imagine the capacity of your digestive system to process food and to draw the goodness out of it for your body needs ... Get in touch with its capacity to eliminate waste ... And again feel God's delight and joy and wonder at the mystery of this part of your body ... and notice how you feel as you experience God saying It is good ... It is very good ...

Then, in your imagination, experience God creating your spine ... your spine with all the many bones connected to one another yet separate ... Become aware of the wonder of this spine with its strength and its flexibility ... as it protects the spinal cord, the carrier of messages throughout the body ... Experience the Spirit creating the tree of nerves that come out from it ... and the rib cage that protects your vital organs ...

Then the Spirit creates the heart ... planting in it the power to pump blood even when you are not aware of it ... Get a sense of the miracle of your heart ... and of the circulatory system with which it connects ... bringing life ... cleansing toxins ... bringing nurture to the tiniest corpuscle of your body ...

And then God creates the lungs to transform the air you breathe into the nurture essential for your body's life ... your lungs that bring the oxygen you need for life ... and that also cleanse poisons that build up ... And as God sees what has been created in delight and joy, God says It is good ... It is very good ...

Next your shoulders and arms ... with bones that are strong and powerful... and with joints that are flexible ... Notice the great miracle that is the creation of your arms and hands ... The complexity of creation that is in just one hand ... the fingers that move ... the power to grasp ... to feel ... to touch ... to lift ... to hold ... to create ... to work ... to play ...

God creates your neck and throat ... and your skull to protect the brain inside ... Imagine the wonder of the brain that is yours ... Imagine its ability to transform messages from the eyes into sight ... messages from the ears into hearing... messages of the soul into feelings ... messages of the mind into thinking ... Imagine its ability to keep going all the unconscious systems of breathing ... and blood circulation ... and digestion ... Imagine its ability to remember ... to organize ... to think ... to process ... to integrate ...

Next God creates your face and your ears and your nose, and your mouth ... and God looks with delight on this you that is a holy creation ... Let the words of God sink deeply into your being ... It is good ... It is very, very good ...

But still there is something missing as God looks at this creation ... And so God breathes God's very Spirit into you ... breathes life into you ... and you come alive to the Spirit ... and to feeling ... to meaning and to love ... You come alive to an awareness of your connection with all of life ... for you share the same breath ... God breathes into you life energy ... and the power to grow, both physically and spiritually ... and the power to heal and to restore balance ... And God dances in delight at this wondrous creation ... It is good ... It is very very good ...

Allow yourself some time to experience yourself as the delight of God ... as the mysterious and miraculous creation of God ... Let the words It is good ... It is very good ... resonate through your whole being ...

Is there anything you want to share with this One that has created you in this way? ... Is there any wisdom your body would like to give you right now? ...

Gradually become aware of your body-self as your are sitting (or lying) ... Begin to notice your breath ... Begin to make some gentle movements with your fingers, and toes, and neck ... When you feel ready open your eyes.

SHARING
JOURNALLING/DRAWING

DEBRIEFING
Ask participants to share what happened for them in the meditation:
- What was God like for you in this meditation?
- What was God doing in and through this experience for you? Was there any wisdom/learning?
- Did you have any resistance to seeing your body-self as good?
- How do you feel about experiencing yourself as a temple of Holiness?

CLOSURE
a) Look at your hands as you might imagine God seeing them. Notice the strength, the intricacy of your hands — of your fingers that can do so many

things. Think of the things your hands are capable of doing: the work of lifting heavy loads, comforting a child, creating beauty, touching with love, fixing what is broken, washing what is soiled, writing messages from the brain, playing a musical instrument, others? Think with awe of all the things your hands have done this week and give thanks. Ask God to bless these hands, created in love.

b) Look at the hands of others in the group as each person holds out their open hands to the centre. Notice the variety of shapes and sizes of hands. Imagine all of the creating activity that has come through these hands in the past week. As you give thanks, ask God to bless the hands of each of those gathered. As the circle breaks up, you might invite participants to allow one another to look at their hands as they offer peace to one another before leaving.

c) Pass the mirror around and invite the participants to look deeply into their own eyes and see themselves as the loving Creator sees them — and to say out loud, "It is good, it is very good" or, as one of the members of our group said, "I am good, I am very good."

MEDITATION

3

THE HEALING POOL

INTRODUCTION

PREPARATION

- paper and pens/pencils/drawing materials
- bowl of water
- candle
- open Bible
- pictures of water

SCRIPTURE: JOHN 5:2–9

This meditation could also be used with the story of Naaman healed of his leprosy, 2 Kings 5:1–14; or the baptism of Jesus, Matthew 3:13–17; or Mark 1:9–11; or Luke 3:21–22.

REFLECTION

In this meditation we will be working with images of healing. I have used this meditation with cancer patients, and with others seeking physical healing. However, it is also useful with those seeking inner emotional and spiritual healing. It is particularly helpful as part of a process of healing of memories. There is increasing interest in the medical profession in the links between mind, spirit, and body. Several books have been written in this area recently.[13]

Our bodies respond physically to the use of imagery. Advertisers know this well. Athletes use meditation to improve their physical performance. Meditation is used in a number of hospitals, particularly in the areas of cancer and AIDS treatment and pain control. It is a powerful tool to promote healing and to help the whole person work with the Source of healing through the body and soul's own healing process.

I think of the power for healing in terms of balancing the energies in a person's body-self with their emotional and spiritual selves. In each of us, I believe, there is an inner healer that can be accessed through prayer, meditation, and practising the Presence of God. Our unconscious minds can both create and heal.

The attitude with which healing meditation is approached, however, is fundamental. It is not a magic cure-all, though physical healing may occur. It is a process, not a one-shot effort. There are many ways in which healing may take place. One person may be healed of her fear of death so that she can die with grace and dignity and in peace when it is her time. Another person may experience healing of life-style. Another may be able to let go of the control certain memories have had on their lives. For another self-acceptance may be the healing. For some, as lives come more into balance, physical healing occurs. For me it is important to let go of expectations for particular results. It is important not to claim or promise results over which one has no control.

GATHERING

a) Think of a time when you have been physically ill.
    - What was going on in your life at the time and in the time just before it?
    - Are you aware of any emotional or spiritual dimensions to this illness?

b) There are studies that have been made of two people who have had identical heart surgery. One is prayed for by a group of people who do not even know the person. Both are given the same medical care. The nursing staff do not know about the experiment but all the medical staff notice a marked im-provement in healing in the one who has been prayed for. What do you make of this?

c) Can you think of a time in your life, or in the life of someone you know, when emotional factors created illness?

d) When Dr. Bernie Siegel begins to deal with a cancer patient, he asks: "What does this illness mean for you? What does this illness allow you to do that you felt you could not do? Are there things in your life that you can change without having to have an illness draw your attention to it?" Do any of these questions have meaning for you?

e)   As you arrive in this place, are you aware of any part of your life that is in need of healing?

MEDITATION

Close your eyes ... Let yourself pay attention to what it feels like to be in this body-self that is you today ... right now ... Most of us go through whole days ... sometimes our whole lives ... without really paying attention to this body-self ... In Hebrew, the language Jesus knew, there was no such thing as disembodied spirit ... They spoke of the *nephesh* ... the body-soul ... the spirit/body ... Jesus talked about our bodies as temples of the Spirit ... What is it like for you to think of yourself in that way?

As you begin to pay attention to your body, do you notice places where tension is stored up? ... where your muscles are in tight knots? ... As you scan your body, from the top of your head to the bottom of your feet ... notice if there are tender places ... .sore spots ... and send compassion to these places in your body, thanking them for the hard work they are doing ... perhaps offering to pay more attention to what they are telling you in the future ...

Become aware of your breathing, this life-sustaining process that goes on all of the time, even when we are unaware ... Notice if you are breathing with only a small part of your lungs, or whether you are taking the breath deeply into your whole being, down to the bottom of your lungs ... up to the tops of your shoulders ... Notice if your tummy moves in and out as you inhale and exhale ... the way a baby's does when it is breathing naturally ...

Notice where you are tightened up ... not fully open to the breath of life ... Let your body relax ... let the tension flow out of your body through your feet ... Begin to allow your breath to move deeper into your being ... taking the breath deep down into your belly ... creating inner space ...

Breathe in deeply the healing presence of the Spirit ... the goodness and grace of God ... Take it right into the core of your being ... As you breathe out, let the breath carry with it the poisons ... physical ... emotional ...

spiritual ... that have built up in your system ... Breathe in possibility ... hope that the Spirit gives ... Let go of the stress and tensions that are stored in your body-self ... your emotional-self ... your spiritual-self ... Breathe in life energy ... The creating breath of God that was there from the beginning ... Breathe out whatever would block you from being fully present to this time ...

Again notice your body ... If there continue to be tense places, imagine the healing breath moving directly to those spots ... unknotting the tension ... letting go ... letting be ... letting open ... letting unlock ... Know that you are in a safe place ... that this is a place where it is safe to be ... Notice the inner space that is being prepared and opened up inside you ... space for the Sacred Presence to find room ... space for the Holy One to be with you ... your own sacred space ... your own holy ground ... Your own sacred centre ...

Imagine yourself in the evening walking in the bright moonlight along a wide path in a beautiful forest ... This is a safe place ... There is nothing to harm you here ... The trees are spaced quite widely so that you can see the sky, the moon, and the beautiful stars ... Walk along the path ... catching the scent of the growing trees ... of the fresh night air ... Come to a clearing that is covered with a lush green grass ... There is a beautiful pool of water in this clearing ... You know that this is a pool whose waters have special healing powers and that there is healing here for you ...

Around the pool are beautiful moist dark green leafy plants ... Some have lovely flowers ... See the colours ... Get a sense of all of the lush growth that is nurtured by these healing waters ... See the full moon with its reflection repeated in the water ... Listen for any sounds ... Experience as fully as you possibly can this wonderful place ... savouring its beauty and its peaceful healing quality ...

You have brought a prayer mat ... a place to encounter the sacred ... and some scented oil in a bowl ... and a candle for lighting ... Light the candle, invoking the light of Christ ... Sit on the mat and be in touch with anything that you feel needs healing in you ... You may wish to invite the Christ or a Healing Spirit to be present with you in some more visible form ... or you may prefer to be alone in the Presence ... It may be a part of your body that is unwell ... It may be a painful memory that has not yet been healed ... It may be how you are behaving in a relationship ... Or some other part of your life that cries out in some way for healing ... Give yourself some time to focus on this ... to find the particular part that is longing for healing ...

Be in touch with your need and your desire for healing ... Be in touch as well with any thing that would hold you back ... but don't dwell on that ... Simply be aware of resistance if there is any ... Let the desire for healing grow in you ... Know that this pool is here for your healing ... that its waters have the power to heal ... When you feel ready to enter the pool, stand up ... and prepare to enter the water ... If you wish you may ask someone to help you ... A someone who would be a healing presence for you ... or you may enter the water alone ...

Allow yourself to enter the water ... Notice how you enter ... Do you go in slowly? ... or quickly? ... Feel the healing power of the water as it touches you ... It has power to heal body ... soul ... feelings ... memories ... Feel its life move in you as you enter it ... Feel it flow over your body ... but also feel it permeating your whole being with its healing, strengthening power ...

Let the alive-ness come to you from this water of life ... Let peace, deep peace come to you from this water of life ... Let the water massage gently the wounded places ... releasing the power for life ... Let the water cleanse the places in you that feel unworthy, unacceptable ... Let the water wash the places where you feel shame ... Let the water pour its life and goodness into your whole being ...

When you feel ready, cup your hands to scoop up the water and say "your name ... I forgive you," as you pour the healing water over your head and face and shoulders ... Do this again saying this time "Your name, I love you" ... Do this several times alternating these words ... using your own name ... pouring the healing, cleansing, life-making waters, over you ... "I forgive you" ... "I love you" ... Take the time you need to do this ...

When you feel that the time is right ... come out of the water ... dry your body if you would like to ... and sit on the prayer rug ...There is perfumed oil there ... If you would like ... use it to anoint yourself ... Dip your fingers in the oil and anoint your forehead ... your eyes ... your lips ... your heart ... your hands ... your feet ... honouring your sacred-self ... claiming the oil of gladness and healing for yourself ...

Conclude your healing in a way that feels right for you ... perhaps with a time of prayer and reflection on what has happened ... Know that you take this healing with you as you leave this place and that it will continue to work in you ...

When you feel ready, walk back to the forest ... Look back and see the healing pool in the moonlight, knowing that you can return there when-ever you need to or want to ... Continue down the path through the forest ... Notice if you feel any different from when you had been approaching the clearing ... When you arrive at the place you began, be in touch again with your body as it is sitting (or lying) ... Notice your breathing ... Make some gentle movements with your fingers and toes ... your neck and shoulders ... When you feel ready, open your eyes ...

SHARING

JOURNALLING/DRAWING

DEBRIEFING

Ask participants to share what happened for them in the meditation:
- What was God like for you in this meditation?
- What was God doing in and through this experience for you?
- Was there any wisdom/learning for you?

CLOSURE

There are several options for a ritual around water or oil that could be significant:

a)   Invite people to go to the centre and, lifting up water in their hands and letting it pour back into the bowl, say out loud the words of the affirmation in the meditation: "Your name I forgive you." Again lifting the water and as it pours into the bowl say "Your name, I love you."

Meditation 3

b)   Pass the water around the circle inviting participants to dip their fingers in it an anoint themselves or each other.

c)   Pass oil in a small bowl around the circle for participants to make the sign of the cross or simply touch it to their forehead, their wrists, their lips, their eyes, any parts of their body that they wish. I use either a perfumed or non-perfumed massage oil or almond oil. These are available in health food stores or in various places where massage oils are sold.

4

THE RIVER OF LIFE

INTRODUCTION

PREPARATION

- paper and pens/pencils/drawing materials
- bowl of water
- photographs of different kinds of rivers

SCRIPTURE: GENESIS 2:4B–14, REVELATION 22:1–5

There are rivers mentioned in scripture from Genesis to Revelation. Genesis 2:4b–14 and Revelation 22:1–5 are powerful primal images of the river of life that flows from the very beginning to the very end. Psalm 46 is also a powerful image of the river of hope and promise. Isaiah 43:18–21 is again an image of God's promise in terms of water and river. There are many other scriptures that could also be appropriate where images of water and of river are used.

REFLECTION

Anyone who has sat beside a flowing river can attest to the power of this experience to calm us into a reflective, meditative state. The river is archetypal imagery for the flow of life, the flow of emotional and spiritual reality.

As you prepare for this meditation I would invite you to remember times when you have sat by a river — to relax, to weep, to contemplate, to celebrate with another.

One powerful experience for me happened while writing this book, in California in Yosemite Park. I was sharing picnic lunch on a large rock in a quickly flowing mountain stream. I found myself looking downstream "towards the future" I told the person who was with me. He was looking in the opposite direction, upstream "towards the future." As we discussed our differing points of view we realized that he was identifying with the rock, seeing the future as the stream coming towards him. I was identifying with the river, in movement flowing towards the sea. This said much about our diverse natures.

There are deep spiritual insights to be gained by attending to the river of life.

GATHERING

a)   When you think of the word "river," what comes to mind?

b)   If you had to describe your life right now as a river, what kind of river would you be? How would you be flowing?

MEDITATION

Shut your eyes and let your body relax ... Let it sink into the chair or into the floor ... Let yourself be held up ... supported by the chair or floor ... You do not need to do the work of holding up your body ... You can let it be supported ... You can let go and relax ...

Begin to notice your breathing ... Breath is essential to living ... It was God's breath, we are told, that created all that is ... It has the power for cleansing and healing not only our physical system ... but also our emotional and spiritual lives ... Notice the breath as it begins at the tip of your nose ... Feel the cool air as it moves through your nostrils ... Follow it as it moves across the roof of your mouth ... Follow it as it goes down into your windpipe ... Follow it as it goes through your bronchial tubes into your lungs ... Notice where it goes into your lungs ... How deeply is the breath of life moving within you? ...

Gradually allow your breath to move more deeply into your being ... Let it open up space inside you ... space to meet the Holy ... space for you to BE ...

Gradually allow yourself to soften and flow with the breath ... Let your shoulders fall and relax as you breathe into the part of your lungs high up in your shoulders ... Let your tummy muscles relax and let go as you let the breath move deeply into your whole torso ... Notice what it feels like to be in your body-self as this happens ... Notice the feeling of letting go ... of relaxing ... of well-being ... of inner space for meeting the Holy ...

Pick one place (either the tip of the nose or a place in the lungs), in which to simply observe the breath as it passes ... in and out ... in and out ... Let yourself come to your sacred centre to the still place inside ...

As you become in touch with the silence within you, imagine yourself walking in a lovely woods ... the sun is shining through the trees ... See its rays as it passes through the openings in the trees ... You notice all of the different types of vegetation ... Notice all of the greens and browns ... all of the other colours that are present in this woods ... Notice the smells of the living, growing power of nature all around you ... Feel the earth under your feet ... Notice if there are any birds or insects or other life in the forest ...

As you follow the path ... come to a river ... Go to a place where you are beside the river and can see clearly both upstream and down stream ... How is the water flowing? ... Is it flowing quickly or slowly? ... Is the current fast or slow? ... Notice the trees and bushes and plants growing alongside the river ... Are there any rocks or other obstacles in the river? ... Notice how the water flows in those places ... Are there places where the river has uprooted shrubs along its banks? ... Is the water clear or is it carrying a lot of stirred up debris with it? ...

Look upstream and get a sense of the river's source ... Follow the river back and notice where it has come from ... Are there other streams that have joined it before it has arrived at the place where you are standing? ...

Now experience the flow of your own life as river ... Is your water cool and clear ... or muddy and warm? ... How deep are you as you experience your-self as river? ... Are you a quickly flowing stream, or a deep wide river? ... What is your bottom like? ... What are the obstacles that block and shape your path? ... What are you carrying with you? ...

Notice where you have been life-giving to what is growing around you ...
How have you been living water to give growth? ... Are there places where
your power has been destructive? ...

Listen for the wisdom that is there for you as you experience yourself as
river ... What feelings arise as the water flow reflects the flow of your life? ...
Where is the source of this river of life for you? ... Where is the source of the
life that is flowing through you now? ... What or who has joined your flow
to make it greater? ... What effect is your life flow having on others? ... on
the earth? ... on other living things? ...

Notice how your colours and flow are affected by what is growing around
you ... Are you the kind of river that children would feel safe playing in? ...
How would you feel about that? ... Is your water refreshing or tasteless? ...
How do you feel about yourself as a river? ...

Now imagine yourself standing beside the river again ... Go to a different
place to get a different vantage point ... Try to get a sense of where this river
is in its full cycle ... Are you standing nearer to the source or to the mouth?
... As you observe the river, has anything changed? ... Ask God's Spirit to
give you any insight that would be important for you to have at this point
in your life ...

Gradually turn and walk back into the forest returning to where you began
.... bring with you the wisdom and insight the Spirit has given you in this
time ...

Slowly come back into touch with your body-self as it is sitting (or lying) ...
Be in touch with your breathing and make some gentle movements with
your body as you begin to return to this place ... Open your eyes when you
feel ready ...

S H A R I N G

Journalling/Drawing
This meditation may lend itself to drawing as a way to ground the meditation before sharing. Whenever I suggest a drawing exercise, I also offer the option of writing, because there are many who feel very insecure and threatened about their artistic abilities.

Debriefing
Ask participants to share what happened for them in the meditation:
- What was God doing in this meditation for you?
- Was there any wisdom or learning for you?

C L O S U R E
Choose one from Chapter 5.

MEDITATION

5

BAPTISM — TRANSFORMATION
— HEALING CHANGE

INTRODUCTION
PREPARATION
- paper and pens/pencils/drawing materials
- bowl of water

SCRIPTURE: MATTHEW 3:13–17, MARK 1:9–11, LUKE 3:21–22

REFLECTION

Jesus was at a turning point in his life. He was about to begin grappling with the meaning of his life. I believe that he, like the rest of us, had to struggle with what that meaning was. I don't see Jesus as a divine puppet simply living out a prearranged plan. I realize that people afterwards, in trying to make sense of the experience, sometimes made it sound that way.

When I had a sense of God's call in my own life, it did not come with a perfectly laid out blueprint and step-by-step instructions. It came as a profound pull in my soul that had to be followed, but it was very much a step into the unknown. The known part was the relationship with Spirit. Where it was leading was pretty hazy. I imagine it was that way for Jesus. He needed to fulfil his life. He felt the Spirit beckoning, drawing him. Yet what direction to take? How to go about it?

I find it fascinating that Jesus' baptism takes place in the wilderness. It is the place one would avoid if one could, the place where danger lurked. And he is baptized by a radical prophetic man, John the Baptizer. John had started a movement that believed that society needed to change to its very roots. Cosmetic changes here and there would not be enough. Those who came to John were dissatisfied with the status quo and were looking for a new way. They responded at the core of their beings to his message that a huge change was coming. They were prepared to offer themselves to that transformation by undergoing the ritual of baptism; a dying to the old, and a rising to the new.

Jesus seems to have felt in solidarity with this movement for he asks John to baptize him as well. But this is only the beginning of the journey. Immediately after his baptism, Jesus is led by the Spirit into the wilderness. Wilderness is a place of testing, of deprivation, and of radical cutting away to the roots of one's being. Jesus is in the desert for forty days and forty nights (a biblical way of saying a long time). Jesus must have struggled with the meaning and direction of his life and of his ministry.

One is reminded of the forty years the Israelites spent wandering in the desert on the freedom road from Egyptian slavery. In scripture, this too was a time of radical formation, of testing of purpose and direction, of creating a new people.

GATHERING

a) Connect with the symbol of water. What comes to your mind as you begin this session?

b) Have you ever been baptized? What does it mean for you?

c) Where do you sense people crying out for a turning around of the direction in which the world is travelling? How do you feel about such people?

d) Remember a time when you have had to struggle with the direction in which your life was going. What kinds of feelings and tensions arose for you?

MEDITATION

Close your eyes ... Let yourself pay attention to what it feels like to be in this body-self that is you today ... right now ... Most of us go through whole days ... sometimes our whole lives ... without really paying attention to this body-self ... In Hebrew, the language Jesus knew, there was no such thing as disembodied spirit ... They spoke of the *nephesh* ... the body-soul ... the spirit/body ... Jesus talked about our bodies as temples of the Spirit ... What is it like for you to think of yourself in that way?

As you begin to pay attention to your body, do you notice places where tension is stored up? ... where your muscles are in tight knots? ... As you scan your body, from the top of your head to the bottom of your feet ... notice if there are tender places ... sore spots ... and send compassion to these places in your body, thanking them for the hard work they are doing ... perhaps offering to pay more attention to what they are telling you in the future ...

Become aware of your breathing, the life-sustaining process that goes on all of the time, even when you are unaware ... Notice if you are breathing with only a small part of your lungs, or whether you are taking the breath deeply into your whole being, down to the bottom of your lungs ... up to the tops of your shoulders ... Notice if your tummy moves in and out as you inhale and exhale ... the way a baby's does when it is breathing naturally ... Notice where you are tightened up ... not fully open to the breath of life ... Let your body relax ... let the tension flow out of your body through your feet ...

Begin to allow your breath to move deeper into your being ... taking the breath deep down into your belly ... creating inner space ... Breathe in deeply the healing presence of the Spirit ... the goodness and grace of God ... Take it right into the core of your being ... As you breathe out, let the breath carry with it the poisons ... physical ... emotional ... spiritual ... that have built up in your system ... Breathe in possibility ... hope that the Spirit gives ... Let go of the stress and tensions that are stored in your body-self ... your emotional-self ... your spiritual-self ... Breathe in life energy ... The creating breath of God that was there from the beginning ... Breathe out whatever would block you from being fully present to this time ...

Again notice your body ... If there continue to be tense places, imagine this healing breath moving directly to this tension ... unknotting it ... letting go ... letting be ... letting open ... letting unlock ...

Know that you are in a safe place ... that this is a place where it is safe to be ... Notice the inner space that is being prepared and opened up inside you ... space for the Sacred Presence to find room ... Space for the Holy One to be with you ... Your own sacred space ... your own holy ground ... Your own sacred centre ...

Imagine yourself walking across a field on a hot afternoon ... smell the dried grasses and the hot dry air ... hear the buzz of the flies ... feel the heat of the sun as it beats down on your body ... Feel your thirst in this dry heat ... You are on a path that is leading to a place you feel drawn to ... though you do not know exactly what you will find there ... Notice the mixture of anticipation ... uncertainty ... that you feel as you continue ... Become aware that there are others on this path ... Notice them ... Speak to them or not as you feel you wish ...

Become aware, the closer you come to this place, that you are coming out of a deep longing for change within you ... Let it rise up in you as you are walking ... this desire for change ... As you become aware of it ... notice if there are any particular areas of your life that seem to cry out for a need for change ... Notice if there are any things in the world and the culture around you that seem to cry out for change ... Take some time to allow the Spirit to offer you the awareness of what needs to change ...

Ahead of you, you see a larger group of people who seem to be stopping in a particular area under some trees ... There seems to be a river there and some shade ... Come to the river and notice that people are listening to one particular person speak about the need for change, change that goes to the very core of things ... What does this person look like? ... What tone of voice is being used to speak to those gathered? ... This person seems to have the words that name your own deepest longings and knowings ...

The words connect with your own experience, and help you clarify your own deep desires for transformation ... You have a sense that this is a prophet or a very holy person ... Notice what this person is saying ... How do you feel about what is being said? ... Is the person speaking about changes on a personal level? ... changes in the society? ... changes in relationships? ... other changes? ...

This person invites everyone to be part of this movement for changing themselves and the way things are ... You are invited to come into the flowing river ... this river of life ... this continually moving water ... to allow the water to flow over your whole body, your whole being ... to allow what needs to die in you to pass away ... to let go of the old distorted way of being ... You are invited to offer yourself to a new way ... to new life ... to transformed life ... Decide how your feel about doing this ... Watch as others enter the waters of the river ... Watch as they go under the water and a blessing is given ...

Feel the desire for change rising in you ... feel any resistance you might have as well ... Are you able to enter the waters of this river to allow their healing, renewing waters to flow over you? ... Are you ready to offer yourself to change? ... to letting go of what needs to be let go ... Are you ready to take on the power of the Spirit in your life? ... Let yourself feel any feelings that arise ... anxiety ... anticipation ... excitement ... fear ... whatever arises for you, simply let it be in you ...

If you feel ready to enter the river ... in spite of any anxieties and concerns you feel ... allow yourself to enter the water ... Feel the flow of the current ... Feel the fresh, cool water on your hot, dusty body as you go into the stream ... Allow yourself to go into the water as deeply as you are able ...

Feel the old, used patterns in your life flowing away with the stream ... Feel the cleansing of the water ... Feel the refreshing, energizing power of these holy waters ... Feel new life rising in you ... Feel the freedom of letting go creating more space inside you ... Feel the energies that you have used to hang on to outworn patterns and thoughts release ... Feel the power that had been locked up in destructive tendencies return to you ... giving you renewed energy for this new being that you are in the process of becoming ... Feel the hope that comes from committing yourself to the new being ...

And then as you rise out of the water let yourself experience what almost seems like a voice ... the presence of the Spirit communicating ... "You are my beloved, the one in whom I delight"... Let yourself experience fully the power of this affirming love of the Spirit ... Let yourself experience God's delight in you ... as God's beloved ... Feel the power of this affirmation from the very core of the universe ... Know that this love is with you in your commitment to new life and to change in yourself and in your world ... Know that it will sustain you in times of trial ... in times of despair ... in times when the going is tough and the vision seems a long way off ... Rest, for as long as you are able, in this delight of God ... Feel its healing power ... Feel its energizing power ... Feel its power to make all things new ... And know that it is in you ...

Then come away from this place, back to the place where you began, as you bring with you the experience you have had at the river ...

Gradually become aware of your body as you are sitting (or lying) ... Notice your breathing ... Make some gentle movements with your fingers ... your toes ... your neck and shoulders ... When you are ready, gradually open your eyes.

SHARING

JOURNALLING/DRAWING

DEBRIEFING

Ask participants to share what happened for them in the meditation:
- What was God doing in this meditation for you?
- Was there any wisdom or learning for you?
- What desire for change did you discover welling up in you?
- Were you able to enter the water? What happened for you then?

CLOSURE

There are several options for a ritual around water that could be significant:

a) Invite participants to come one by one to do what they would like to do with the bowl of water. Some may make the cross on their forehead. Others will dip their fingers in the water and put it on other parts of their body. Some will run their fingers through the water, or let it flow down over their hands and fingers. Some will offer to anoint another. Some will splash. It is amazing to see what people do totally naturally in a ritual act.

b)   Another option would be to be more directive and suggest what participants might do with the water. You could suggest that they put water on the forehead of the person next to them or on their own forehead.

c)   Another option would be for the person facilitating to take a branch of a living tree (cedar works well) and sprinkle those gathered. This is an ancient ritual to remind Christians of their baptism. The cedar is one of the sacred herbs in Aboriginal tradition connected with healing and life.

d)   Sing: Spirit of the Living God or Shall We Gather at the River.

6

I AM THE VINE,
YOU ARE THE BRANCHES

INTRODUCTION

PREPARATION

- paper and pens/pencils/drawing materials
- growing plant with well developed branches
- fruit or flowers

SCRIPTURE: JOHN 15:1–5, GENESIS 2:1–9, LUKE 13:6–9

REFLECTION

The passage from John is one of Jesus' I AM sayings. Those familiar with the Hebrew language, would make the link with the NAME YHWH, given to Moses at the burning bush. While difficult to translate into English, it means I am who I am, or I will be who I will be, or I am Being-ness Becoming. For John, Jesus was nothing less than a manifestation of this mystery of Being-ness.

In this meditation we use the image of God as gardener as well as imagery around the vine and the process of growth and care. This imagery would also work well with some of the early stories in Genesis or with the parable of the barren fig tree in Luke. In this meditation, we look at what helps and what hinders or restricts our growth.

Each of us knows that there are certain periods of our lives, often when we are in transition or have changing circumstances, that we are opened to more and deeper levels of transformation. At other times, we lie fallow and gather energy inwardly for the next stage of outward growth. Many factors create the climate for growth, just as many factors challenge and even block it. To use the imagery of the scripture, sometimes the soil needs to be enriched and cared for to sustain our growth. Sometimes we recognize the need to put down new and deeper roots for change to occur. Sometimes we need water, or sun. Other times there are destructive patterns that need to be cut out.

Perhaps one of the most important aspects of this meditation on growth is the acknowledgement that there are needs that we cannot meet all by ourselves. We have, it seems to me, to find the healthy balance between two opposite poles that are not particularly helpful.

At the one extreme, there has been in Christian history an unhealthy, disempowering strand of theology that has had participants confess to being worms, needing salvation completely from outside. In this theological stance it is as if we humans are powerless to do anything for ourselves, and unworthy to dare even to expect anything good to happen for us.

At the other extreme, in the culture there has been a tendency, even in much of the personal growth movement, to suggest that we are personally responsible for all of our emotional and physical well-being, and that we can do it all ourselves. I believe that, while we have to unleash every bit of the human potential that is inherent in our God-given power, we also need to be able to let go to the Other — to trust in the ultimate caring of God's Spirit, or as it is imaged here, the Gardener. This in fact becomes the supportive groundwork out of which a person feels centred and strong enough to take on their personal responsibility for their path of growth. Discerning where the gardener is working in our lives can strengthen and enhance our spiritual and emotional growth.

For many of us, allowing ourselves to trust the gardener is incredibly difficult. Real resistance arises. In debriefing the meditation, it is useful for each person to explore the nature of any resistance and fear of trusting that is experienced. This is an key part of the spiritual journey. Many of us will go without the necessary care, nurture, and tending we both need and long for, because we are too afraid to trust that it might actually be there. This kind of poverty thinking can become a very constricting box that limits our vision of what we believe is possible for our lives. We can only create what we can envision.

There is, in many people's experience, history that gets triggered by the invitation to trust. It evokes past hurts, fear of abandonment, fear of being over-powered, fear of losing control, fear that it will turn out to be a hoax, as it has been in other times in the past when we have tried to reach out. There are also all of the messages we have learned about the need to be self-sufficient, and to look after our own needs.

Many of us have been taught that we are selfish to think about our own needs. We have not always been sophisticated enough in our spirituality to distinguish between ego-centred needs and needs of the core-self, the emerging sacred-self God created us to be. When we do not pay attention to the needs for growth and spiritual nurture and care of this core-self, we are thwarting God's presence and power in our lives.

There is so much unlearning that must take place for growth in the Spirit. I sometimes wonder if this is what Jesus meant suggesting that a little child was closer to the reign of God than the righteous religious adults to whom he was speaking. The child does not have so much to unlearn and, I hope, is not afraid to ask for what she or he needs.

I remember my mother as the gardener in our family, constantly and faithfully trying to get fruitfulness out of clay soil that was not the greatest for growing things. When I picture the gardener in meditation, she has often come to mind. For others in our meditation group images of the gardener have been Jesus, an old farmer, a child, a spouse, a sense of the Spirit tending. God has a great resourcefulness when it comes to reaching us in ways we can be touched.

GATHERING

You may want to share some of the ideas in the reflection as you begin.

a)   As you think about gardens, or plants you have grown in your home, is there any wisdom that you have learned from them?

b)   Try to remember the first garden you ever experienced. Try to recapture the feeling of being in it. Who looked after it? What did it grow?

c)   If you were thinking about your life as a garden right now, what would it look like?
   - What season would it be?
   - How is the garden of your life growing right now?
   - What might it need to help it grow better?

MEDITATION

Shut your eyes and let your body relax ... let it sink into the chair or into the floor ... Let yourself be held up ... supported by the chair or floor ... You do not need to do the work of holding up your body ... you can let it be supported ... you can let go and relax ... Begin to notice your breathing ... Breath is essential to living ... We are told in scripture that it was God's breath that created all that is ... It has the power for cleansing and healing

... not only our physical system ... .but also our emotional and spiritual lives ... Notice the breath as it begins at the tip of your nose ... Feel the cool air as it moves through your nostrils ... Follow it as it moves across the roof of your mouth ... Follow it as it goes down into your windpipe ... Follow it as it goes through your bronchial tubes into your lungs ... Notice where it goes in your lungs ... How deeply is the breath of life moving within you? ... Gradually allow your breath to move more deeply in your body ... Let it open up space inside you ... space to meet the Holy ... space for you to BE ...

Gradually allow yourself to soften and flow with the breath ... Let your shoulders fall and relax as you breathe into the part of your lungs high up in your shoulders ... Let your tummy muscles let go as you let the breath move deeply into your whole torso ... Notice what it feels like to be in your body-self as this happens ...

Now move through your body tensing and letting go of the muscles ... Begin with your feet ... Tense the muscles of your feet then let go ... Experience what it feels like to let go and to relax ... Move up to the calves ... tense ... hold tight ... then relax ... let go ... Move up to the thighs ... tense ... hold tight ... then relax ... let go ... Move to the hips and pelvis ... tense ... hold tight ... then relax ... let go ... to the abdomen ... the stomach and middle back ... tense ... hold tight ... then relax ... let go ... to the upper back... tense ... hold tight ... then relax ... let go ... to the shoulders ... the arms ... the hands ... tense ... hold tight ... then relax ... let go ... to the neck ... the head ... tense ... hold tight ... then relax ... let go ...

Notice the feeling of letting go... of relaxing ... of well-being ... Let the breath move freely and deeply into your body ... Let yourself come to your sacred centre ... to the still place inside ... to the inner space for meeting the Holy...

Imagine that you are in a garden, a garden that contains vines. Notice the colours and the feel of the garden ... Is the sun shining? ... Can you feel the temperature of the air on your skin? ... Now imagine you are looking at a vine with many branches ... Look at it closely in your mind's eye ... Notice the colours ... Notice the whole being-ness of this plant ... the odour ... the textures of the leaves ... the older gnarled part of the trunk ... the branches of new life that have come in that year ... the fruit that is forming ... Where is the vine planted? ... Is it a sunny or shady place? ... What kind of soil is the vine planted in? ... How big is the vine? ... How widely does it spread out? ... Is this vine standing alone? ... or are there other vines around? ...

Now become the vine ... to imagine yourself ... and feel yourself as this vine ... Take some time to become aware of yourself as vine ... Experience the kind of soil that you are in ... and how it contains or holds you ... Notice as well if the soil restricts you ... Experience your roots as they reach down into the soil ... Are they strong and firmly anchored to the soil? ... Are they intertwined with other roots? ... Are other plants encroaching on you ... taking moisture and nourishment from you? ... Do you need to put down new and stronger roots? ... reaching further down to get what you need? ...

Experience your main stalk ... Is it strong and capable of carrying the life from the earth? ... Experience the vitality and growing energy that is happening in you ... the energy that comes through you from the earth to bring life and growth ... Become aware of the branches that come out from your central vine ... Feel the growth and the greenness of the life flowing through you ... Be aware of any buds that are about to burst into growth ... So many branches ... Take a good look at all of the branches ... Notice the fruit that is already formed ... Notice the fruit that is forming ... the fruit that is ripening in you ... How much fruit is there? ... Is it healthy? ...

As you are in touch with yourself as the vine, are there any parts of the vine that are sick? ... that have become dead? ... that have become prey to parasites or mould? ... Are there parts where growth has been stunted? ... Are there parts that need pruning to allow for the growth and health of the vine? ... Are there parts that are growing too wildly ... taking too much energy from the whole vine, so that not all parts of the vine can get the nurture they need? ... Be in touch with your needs as a vine ... your need for nourishment ... your need for space to grow ... for water ... for healthy air ... for sun ... for well-tended soil ... your need to have your sickness cared for before it destroys you ...

Experience your need for a gardener ... for one who will care for you ...
watch and protect your growth ... nurture you ... deal with your sickness
and dead parts ... Experience also any resistance and mistrust you might
feel ... Allow your needs to increase so that you overcome your mistrust of
the gardener ... Let yourself experience the nourishment ... the care ... the
healing ... the protection ... that come from this gardener ... Feel the gardener's delight in your growth ... and the gardener's encouragement of your
growing ... Experience the gardener's wisdom in knowing what is needed ...

Experience what happens to you as you allow the gardener to care for you ...
What is it that the gardener needs to do for your healthy growth right now?
... Can you let that happen? ... What feelings arise? ... As you allow the life
force for growing and healing to be strengthened in you ... allow the gardener to let you know the depth of the care that is there for you ...

Gradually draw yourself back to being your body-self ... Become aware
again of your breathing ... Make some gentle movements with your body as
you begin to connect ... Gently and gradually bring yourself back to this
place ... As you feel ready ... open your eyes.

SHARING
JOURNALLING/DRAWING

DEBRIEFING
Ask participants to share what happened for them in the meditation:
 • What did it feel like to experience your need for a gardener?
 • What did the gardener need to do for your growth?
 • Does this ring true for your conscious experience of what you need?

CLOSURE
Choose one from Chapter 5.

MEDITATION

7

YOU ARE LIGHT
FOR ALL THE WORLD

INTRODUCTION

This section contains two meditations on the theme of light, so the scriptures, preparation, reflection, etc. are basically the same. Meditation A allows us to bathe in the healing light of Christ and to offer that healing light to others. Meditation B invites us to allow the light to illuminate the hidden places in us, and to be the light of the world.

PREPARATION

- paper and pens/pencils/drawing materials
- oil lamp, especially a middle-eastern one, on a stand of some sort, perhaps a bushel basket

SCRIPTURE: MATTHEW 5:14–16, JOHN 8:12

REFLECTION

It is hard for those of us who live with street lights and electricity in our homes to begin to imagine the power of the image of light to people in Jesus' time. Remember what happens when the electricity goes out unexpectedly in your home to enter somewhat into the importance of light in darkness.

Light can be a beacon to warn of danger, or to show the direction to go. It can also make visible the unknown, and help to see what is really there. In this way it can dispel unfounded fear, and it can empower a person to deal with what is really dangerous. What we can see clearly and talk about is already less threatening. Light can warm, and it can draw people together, as at a candlelight dinner or around an open fire.

Many people's spirits are affected, like plants, by the amount of light they receive. Modern medicine has recognized seasonal affective disorder (SAD) as directly connected to lessening light and increased darkness in the winter season.

The image of light has been a symbol of the Holy or some aspect of the Holy throughout history. Jesus called himself the Light of the World. He called his followers the Light of the World. Many hymns, poems, prayer, meditations have been created around this very primal image.

GATHERING

a) Remember a time when you were caught in the darkness unexpectedly. What were the feelings?

b) Remember yourself as a child. How did you feel about the dark?

c) Can you think of a person, or persons who have been light in your life; to show the way ahead; to expose dangers; to let you see what was real and what was not?

MEDITATION

A   BATHING IN THE LIGHT OF CHRIST

Shut your eyes and let your body relax ... Let it sink into the chair or into the floor ... Let yourself be held up ... supported by the chair or floor ... You do not need to do the work of holding up your body ... You can let it be supported ... You can let go and relax ...

Begin to notice your breathing ... Breath is essential to living ... It was God's breath, we are told, that created all that is ... It has the power for cleansing and healing not only our physical system ... but also our emotional and spiritual lives ... Notice the breath as it begins at the tip of your nose ... Feel the cool air as it moves through your nostrils ... Follow it as it moves across the roof of your mouth ... Follow it as it goes down into your windpipe ... Follow it as it goes through your bronchial tubes into your lungs ... Notice where it goes into your lungs ... How deeply is the breath of life moving within you? ...

Gradually allow your breath to move more deeply into your being ... Let it open up space inside you ...space to meet the Holy ... space for you to BE ...

Gradually allow yourself to soften and flow with the breath ... Let your shoulders fall and relax as you breathe into the part of your lungs high up in your shoulders ... Let your tummy muscles relax and let go as you let the breath move deeply into your whole torso ... Notice what it feels like to be in your body-self as this happens ... Notice the feeling of letting go ... of relaxing ... of well-being ... of inner space for meeting the Holy ...

Pick one place (either the tip of the nose or a place in the lungs) in which to simply observe the breath as it passes ... in and out ... in and out ... Let yourself come to your sacred centre to the still place inside ...

Imagine yourself sitting on a secluded beach on a sunny afternoon ... You are in a safe place ... Get in touch with the sound of the lapping waves ... the gentle breeze on your skin ... the warmth of the sun as it radiates its healing light on your body ... Feel the living energy that comes from the sun ... awakening your own energy fields ... Get a sense of how the healing light of the sun radiates and evokes life for all the plants and other created life around you ...

Imagine the healing energy of the light of Christ beaming on you through those rays ... Let yourself be bathed and your whole body-self infused with this loving, healing, energizing light of Christ ... Imagine it flowing into your heart ... opening up your feelings ... healing heart wounds ... tenderly massaging tight places that have become knotted through remembered pain ... Imagine it creating space for receiving and giving unconditional love ... as it releases fear and lack of trust ... Let whatever is being released by the presence of the healing light flow out of you ... Imagine it leaving your body to be transformed in the Christ light ...

In your mind's eye, sense the light of Christ moving through your head ... bringing healing to your patterns of thinking ... pouring healing light through your memories ... bathing them, releasing what can be released ... bringing a sacred wholeness to all that it touches ... Feel the light flowing through how you look at the world ... at other people ... Feel the light bathing the way you hear ... the way you take in information ... Feel the light strengthening your power to speak ... the way you express your truth ... with clarity and love ...

Imagine the light moving down through the rest of your body ... bathing your being in the light of Christ ... Move through your torso ... into your abdomen ... Many of us have knots in our bellies where we have stored up swallowed anger, swallowed fear, swallowed pain ... Notice if there are places where you have become diseased or are locked in pain ... places in your body where you have stored up unhealed memories ... Allow the light of Christ to bathe and heal and release those places in the way that is appropriate at this time ...

Allow the light of the Spirit to move down through your legs so that you experience being grounded on the earth ...centred and supported on the good earth...

Feel the enlivening presence of the light in every pore of your being ... Feel the renewing of your spirit ... the releasing of tension ... of pain ... of suffering ... Feel all parts of your being oriented in this light towards healing ... towards living-ness ... towards the love of God ...

Imagine this light flowing both within you ... but also surrounding you ... enveloping you with Christ's protective healing energy ... restoring your body ... your spirit ... your soul ... to its connection with the healing love of the Creator ... Rest in this light for as long as you wish ...

You may wish to continue your mediation by channelling this healing presence and power to a person for whom you wish to pray ... In your mind's eye, bring to awareness the person for whom you wish to pray ... try to get as clear a picture, or sense of the other's presence as possible ... As you continue to experience the light of Christ surrounding you and flowing through you ... get a sense of offering this healing light to the other ... Imagine it flowing through you as you offer it to the other person ...

You may wish to imagine yourself touching the other with healing hands ... or to visualize the light flowing through your heart as you offer it ... image the light surrounding the other in love ... flowing into their being ... bathing the other with its healing and life-giving energy ... Imagine the other person experiencing the wellness, the relaxation, the strengthening of the light of Christ ... Bathe their physical being ... Bathe their emotional and spiritual selves in this healing light ... Offer them and their healing to the Spirit...

When you have done this for as long as feels appropriate ... you might wish to follow the same process for another in need of your healing prayer ... take as long as you need to do this ... Know that as you offer the light through you, you also receive and are renewed ...

Rest in this light for as long as you wish ... Gradually, as you are ready, slowly and gently return to this place, feeling the wholeness you have received in your body ... your mind ... your spirit ... Make gentle movements with your fingers and toes to reconnect you with your body ... Take some conscious deep breaths to reconnect you with your breathing ... As you return, know that you bring with you the healing you have experienced, and that you can return to this place when you wish ... Open your eyes when you are ready.

SHARING

JOURNALLING/DRAWING

DEBRIEFING
Ask participants to share what happened for them in the meditation:
- How did you experience the light?
- Did you become aware of any healing work that God calls you to at this time?
- What was the Spirit like for you in this meditation?

C L O S U R E

a) Make a circle, place hands left palm down, right palm up and place your hand just about an inch from the hand of the person next to you. Pass the light and healing energy around the circle — first to the right — then to the left. Say a closing prayer thanking God for the healing presence of the Spirit.

b) You may also wish to sing one of the following: Spirit of Life; Amazing Grace; Lead, Kindly Light (verse 1); Eternal Light, Shine in My Heart (verse 1); Sending you Light.

M E D I T A T I O N
B   LIGHT TO ALL IN THE HOUSE

Close your eyes ... Let yourself pay attention to what it feels like to be in this body-self that is you today ... right now ... Most of us go through whole days ... sometimes our whole lives ... without really paying attention to this body-self ... In Hebrew, the language Jesus knew, there was no such thing as disembodied spirit ... They spoke of the *nephesh* ... the body-soul ... the spirit/body ...

As you begin to pay attention to your body, do you notice places where tension is stored ... where your muscles are in tight knots? ... As you scan your body, from the top of your head to the bottom of your feet ... notice if there are tender places ... sore spots ... and send compassion to these places in your body, thanking them for the hard work they are doing ... perhaps offering to pay more attention to what they are telling you in the future ... Become aware of your breathing, this life-sustaining process that goes on all of the time, even when we are unaware ... Notice if you are breathing with only a small part of your lungs, or whether you are taking the breath deeply into your whole being, down to the bottom of your lungs ... up to the tops of your shoulders ... Notice if your tummy moves in and out as you inhale and exhale ... the way a baby's does when it is breathing naturally ...

Notice where you are tightened up ... not fully open to the breath of life ... Let your body relax ... let the tension flow out of your body through your feet. ... Begin to allow your breath to move deeper into your being ... taking the breath deep down into your belly ... creating inner space ... Breathe in deeply the healing presence of the Spirit ... the goodness and grace of God ... Take it right into the core of your being ... As you breathe out, let the breath carry with it the poisons ... physical ... emotional ... spiritual ... that have built up in your system ... Breathe in possibility ... hope that the Spirit gives ... Let go of the stress and tensions that are stored in your body-self ... your emotional-self ... your spiritual-self ... Breathe in life energy... the creating breath of God that was there from the beginning ... Breathe out whatever would block you from being fully present to this time ...

Again notice your body ... If there continue to be tense places, imagine this healing breath moving directly to those spots ... unknotting the tension ... letting go ... letting be ... letting open ... letting unlock ... Notice the inner space that is being prepared and opened up inside you ... space for the Sacred Presence to find room ... Space for the Holy One to be with you ... Your own sacred space ... your own holy ground ... Your own sacred centre ...

In your imagination, visualize yourself walking outside, coming to a house just as evening is falling ... Notice what kind of house it is ... Is it small or large? ... Is it well-looked after or unkempt? ... This house is yours ... even though you may not be familiar with it ...

Go up to the door and open it and notice how much darker the interior is than the evening outside ... You can not make out clearly the odd shapes in the room ... You are not really sure what they are ... Feel the uneasiness ... the discomfort ... the anxiety of being in a place where you are not able to see clearly ... Notice what happens to your imagination as it works on shapes that are not clear ... Notice how it feels to be uncertain where it is safe to walk ...

There is no electricity, but as you put your hands out in front of you to make sure that you do not bump into anything, you find a lamp ... Light it and notice what happens ... Notice how it illuminates the room ... Notice how the single flame spreads light far out of proportion to its size ... Notice how it helps you see what the unknown shapes are ... How does this affect your feelings about being in the house? ...

Explore the surroundings, noticing what is there, aware that without the light you would not be able to see any of this house or the things that are in it ... Notice what you are drawn to in the house ...Does this house seem well or poorly furnished? ... Does it feel cluttered or ordered? ...Does it feel warm and inviting, or cold and austere? ...

Notice if there is any way that the lamp can give more light ... What happens when the light is placed higher? ... What would happen to this light if it were placed under a pail? ... What would happen if it were hidden behind a piece of furniture? ...

Imagine this light being the light of Christ's presence ... allow this healing light to bring its healing, enlightening presence into your whole being to explore and light up the house that is you ... Let that light radiate the warmth of healing presence for you ... Notice the colour of the light ... Is the light intense or diffused? ... Feel the energizing power of this light, knowing that it bears the healing presence of the Spirit ...

Centre your attention on your heart, centre of the capacity to give and receive love ... centre of your ability to be open to others ...Take this healing light into your heart centre ... As you allow light to penetrate the darkness in this area of your life, what do you notice? ... What does the light reveal to you? ...

Imagine the light going into your mind and helping you explore your thought processes ... Is your mind clear or cluttered? ... Are there corners there that you did not know about? ... What does the light reveal to you? ...

Imagine it lighting up your feelings, helping you see what you could not see before ... What do you notice? ... Imagine it lighting up your personality ... showing you different sides of yourself? ... Take the time you need to do this.

Now imagine the light lighting up your personal story going through the various stages of your life ... Helping you see more clearly the things you had not noticed before ... Ask that you see only what is there for your healing ... There may be parts that you are not ready or able to see at this time ...

Imagine the light filling your whole being so that you radiate the light too ... Experience the warmth and the light and its burning brightness within you ...

Experience the power that is there to illuminate ... to give light and clarity ... to help others see ... Imagine yourself with someone you love as you allow this light to flow through you to the other ... as you offer freely this light ... Notice anything that happens ...

Imagine yourself with your family or with close friends as one in whom the light is glowing brightly ... How do these people make use of your brightness and warmth? ... How are they affected by it? ...

Imagine yourself in your community doing what you do, bearing this light ... What happens to those around you? ... What happens to your flame? ... Is it burning brightly enough or is it timid and hiding? ...

How do you experience yourself as a lighted flame? ... How brightly do you burn? ... How much do you allow yourself to be seen by others? ... How much do you share your light with others? ... For whom are you a source of light? ... Who shares and enjoys your light and brightness? ...

Bring to mind some of the people touched by your light, seeing them in your mind's eye ... Are there those who live in darkness who need to see your light? ...

Ask God to continue to give light to you ... to continue to bring to light the shadow parts of your own life ... to continue to help you know where your light is shining and needs to shine for others ...

Gradually become aware of yourself as you are sitting (or lying) ... Notice your breathing ... make some gentle movements with your fingers and toes and head ... When you are ready, open your eyes.

S H A R I N G

JOURNALLING/DRAWING

DEBRIEFING

Ask participants to share what happened for them in the meditation:
- What did you discover in this inner journey?
- Jesus called his followers the light of the world. What does being the light of the world mean to you?
- How does it feel to be called that?

C L O S U R E

a) A Body Blessing (see Chapter 5).

b) Song: God is Passionate Life; Lead, Kindly Light (verse 1); Eternal Light, Shine in My Heart (verse 1); Sending you Light.

MEDITATION

8

---◆---

THE HEALING
OF BLIND BARTIMAEUS

INTRODUCTION

PREPARATION
- paper and pens/pencils/drawing materials
- candle
- magnifying glass or a pair of glasses to symbolize sight
- a piece of woven material to symbolize the cloak Bartimaeus throws off

SCRIPTURE: MARK 10:46–52

REFLECTION

The healing stories of Jesus have often been dismissed by rational scientific readers as almost embarrassing superstitious nonsense that can be ignored. They have often been rationalized, explained away, or simply written off. Increasingly as we explore non-traditional healing, and as we understand the link between the body and the mind/spirit, we realize that there is still much mystery.[14] Some of the healing techniques used in Reiki, breath work, Huna, Neurolinguistic Programming, and other body work have remarkable resonance with Jesus' healing.

Though we need to be careful not use healing meditation exercises in a way that would suggest that someone with an organic illness might expect a miraculous physical cure, we can encourage openness to God's healing presence. When we enter these stories in a symbolic, mythical way, we often find surprising power for healing. Sometimes that healing might have physical manifestations, but healing works on many levels. There is healing of attitudes, healing of patterns of living, healing of relationship, healing of self-image, healing of fear, healing of alienation, healing of memories.

In the story of the blind beggar Bartimaeus, we discover, as we often do around Jesus' healing stories, that there is conflict. There are those who do not want the healing to happen. There are those who would try to keep the person in need from growing into a healed, whole-self. Those who would block the healing do not always act this way because they do not wish well for the afflicted person. Rather they support the status quo because they can not imagine that things could be different.

There are those who saw not the person Bartimaeus, but only his disability. They could not see a man who had aspirations and desires. All they could see was a beggar who was blind — both signs in the cultural norm that the person was unfavoured by God. Illness was seen as the result of sin. Lest we think that we have moved far beyond this, in our so-called sophisticated culture, in giving pastoral care I still hear "What have I done to deserve this?" or "Why is God punishing me?"

Bartimaeus refuses to accept the categories into which he has been placed. Instead, in order to get to Jesus and to ask for healing, he throws away his cloak — the one possession he had, his shelter against the cold of night, his protection. He breaks through the barriers of the more "important" people from the town who want to shut him up. Where did he get this kind of power to assert his needs?

GATHERING

a) Ask participants to close their eyes and walk around the room for a few minutes. Invite them to share what that felt like for them.

b) Read the scripture slowly. Reflect on the action of Bartimaeus in throwing off his cloak:
    • Where do you think his power to claim his need and right to healing came from?
    • Where have you found courage to act assertively in the face of opposition?

c) Why do you think the people tried to keep Bartimaeus from Jesus? Have you ever had any supposedly well-meaning friends or relatives try to keep you from asking for what you needed?

MEDITATION

Close your eyes ... Let yourself pay attention to what it feels like to be in this body-self that is you today ... right now ... Most of us go through whole days ... sometimes our whole lives ... without really paying attention to this body-self ... In Hebrew, the language Jesus knew, there was no such thing as disembodied spirit ... They spoke of the *nephesh* ... the body-soul ... the spirit/body ... Jesus talked about our bodies as temples of the Spirit ... What is it like for you to think of yourself in that way?

As you begin to pay attention to your body, do you notice places where tension is stored up? ... where your muscles are in tight knots? ... As you scan your body, from the top of your head to the bottom of your feet ... notice if there are tender places ... sore spots ... and send compassion to these places in your body, thanking them for the hard work they are doing ... perhaps offering to pay more attention to what they are telling you in the future ...

Become aware of your breathing, this life-sustaining process that goes on all of the time, even when you are unaware ... Notice if you are breathing with only a small part of your lungs, or whether you are taking the breath deeply into your whole being, down to the bottom of your lungs ... up to the tops of your shoulders ... Notice if your tummy moves in and out as you inhale and exhale ... the way a baby's does when it is breathing naturally ...

Notice where you are tightened up ... not fully open to the breath of life ... Let your body relax ... let the tension flow out of your body through your feet ... Begin to allow your breath to move deeper into your being ... taking the breath deep down into your belly ... creating inner space ...

Breathe in deeply the healing presence of the Spirit ... the goodness and grace of God ... Take it right into the core of your being ... As you breathe out, let the breath carry with it the poisons ... physical ... emotional ... spiritual ... that have built up in your system ... Breathe in possibility ... Breathe in the hope that the Spirit gives ... Let go of the stress and tensions that are stored on your body-self ...in your emotional-self ... in your spiritual-self ... Breathe in life energy ... the creating breath of God that was there from the beginning ... Breathe out whatever would block you from being fully present to this time ...

Again notice your body ... If there continue to be tense places, imagine this healing breath moving directly to those spots. ... unknotting the tension ... letting go ... letting be ... letting open ... letting unlock ... Know that you are in a safe place ... that this is a place where it is safe to be ... Notice the inner space that is being prepared and opened up inside you ... space for the Sacred Presence to find room ... Space for the Holy One to be with you ... Your own sacred space ... your own Holy ground ... Your sacred centre.

Enter the story of Bartimaeus as you imagine what it would be like to be Bartimaeus, the blind beggar, In your mind's eye, for that is the only eye a blind person has ... imagine yourself sitting on the side of the main dusty road of Jericho ... a busy town ... The sun is beating down ... and there is a lot of noise around you ... Some of the sounds you recognize as familiar ... Others you strain to grasp understanding of what it might be about ... Get in touch with what it would be like to be poor ...without power and security ... without sight ... When you open your eyes you see nothing but darkness ... How would you know when you woke up if it were night or day? ... How does it feel to be blind? ... Experience the darkness within and around you ... Imagine not being able to see where you were walking ... who was coming towards you ... whether you were in danger ... where something was that you had dropped ... Imagine yourself expecting to be blind till death ... What feelings arise in you as you accept this reality? ...

Imagine what in your life might have led you to being a beggar ... Imagine how you are treated by family ... by people in the street ... Imagine what it would be like to live every day of your life knowing that others thought your blindness was a curse from God ...

As you get in touch with yourself as the blind beggar, be on that hot dusty road for a while ... Who pays attention to you? ... What kinds of things do people say to you? ... You begin to hear a different kind of noise, with your ears so highly sensitive to changing sounds ... There seems to be a crowd coming down the road ... You hope it is not a group of Roman soldiers ... You ask someone, "What is happening?" ... "Who is coming?" ... They say that it is that Rabbi from Nazareth ... Jesus they think his name is ... You know who Jesus is ... You've heard about him from the street people who always seem to have the latest news ... You've heard he has healing powers ... This could be your chance to be healed! ...

What longings and needs rise up in you ... Let your desire for healing grow to the point of overwhelming you ... as you await the arrival of the group with Jesus ... Let the impossible hope for wholeness scream out from the centre of your soul ... Let your need for healing explode within you ... as you are driven by a force inside you to rise up ... to cry out ... to beg as you have never begged before ... for all you life depends on it ...

Feel the others in the crowd tell you to shut up ... to be silent ... to stay in your place ... What would be your normal reaction to this? How do you usually react if people are annoyed with you? ... That day the beggar Bartimaeus will not be silent ... You scream out even louder, with a cry that comes from the very depths of your soul ... "Jesus ... Healer ... see me ... heal me ... have mercy" ... The others try to push you into silence ... but your desire for healing is stronger than the fear of rejection ... stronger than your concern for what others think ... Then you realize that the group has stopped right in front of you ... You feel it with your heightened senses ...

You throw off your cloak ... the only possession you have and you leap through the crowd to Jesus who is calling you ... Jesus asks ... "What do you want me to do for you?" ... You are shocked that he asks a blind beggar what he needs ... No one has ever asked you that before ... What do you reply? ... As you are in the presence of Christ ... who is giving you attention and asking the question "What do you want me to do for you?" what do you answer? ... what do you need? ... As you put your needs before Christ, what happens? ... What is Jesus saying to you? ...

Let yourself experience Christ's desire to heal you ... to offer you what you need ... What healing do you receive? ... Bartimaeus was given sight in the story ... Imagine your eyes opened to see ... Imagine the light beginning to come ... Imagine the colours and the shapes ... What is happening in the crowd? ... How are they reacting? ... What is happening in you? ... What is happening with Christ? ... Take the time you need to be with this moment of healing ...

What do you want to do now that this has happened to you? ... What feelings arise as a result of your healing? ... What will this mean for your life? ... Look at Christ as you reflect on these questions and allow dialogue to emerge ...

Now come back into an awareness of being yourself, not Bartimaeus ... Reflect on what the experience of Bartimaeus has to say in your own life? ... Where does it connect with you? ... Where are you able to cry out for what you need? ...What might you need to throw off to risk reaching out for it? ...What would risking healing mean for your life? ... How would it change your life? ...

When you are ready ... gradually and gently draw yourself back to this place ... back to this body-self ... back to your breathing ... And when you are ready ... open your eyes ... and look around you as if you are seeing for the first time.

SHARING
JOURNALLING/DRAWING

DEBRIEFING
Ask participants to share what happened for them in the meditation as they feel comfortable. If you need leading questions, the last two paragraphs of the meditation provide some good jumping off points.

CLOSURE

a)   If a number of participants have had strong experiences around the image of the casting off of the cloak, I might do a sentence completion exercise such as: "In order for me to reach out for what I need for healing, I release ...."

b)   Sing the first verse of "Open My Eyes That I May See."

9

HEALING THE REJECTED PARTS
OF OURSELVES
THE WOMAN WHO BLED FOR TWELVE YEARS

INTRODUCTION
PREPARATION
- paper and pens/pencils/drawing materials
- mirror

SCRIPTURE: MARK 5:21–43

REFLECTION

In Mark's rendition of Jesus' ministry, Jesus has just come from an unclean land healing the mentally ill Legion, who has been living among the dead in the cemetery. He has dealt with pigs — animals that were considered unclean. Now he returns to the other side of the lake, again to heal one who was an outsider, considered unclean.

As embarrassed and uncomfortable as modern western Christians might be to talk of menstrual blood, we have a hard time imagining how startling and outrageous this story would have been to its listeners in Jesus' time. The law taught that blood, particularly menstrual blood was unclean. It taught that the bed a bleeding woman slept on was unclean, the furniture she touched was unclean and a man who touched anything that she had touched was unclean. No one would come to her house. She could not even go to the market without people moving away because her touch was considered to be defiling. She would not even have access to spiritual help at the synagogue or from any Rabbi because she was unclean.

She had done everything she could do to rid herself of this affliction. Her whole savings had been poured out in paying doctors who only seemed to take her money, but not make her well. One might imagine the indignity of some of the treatments they might have tried. Imagine how this would have affected her life and her relationships. It had marked every aspect of her living, her relating, her capacity to be free and fully alive.

Touching Jesus was a sinful act that could have resulted in her being stoned. In doing it, she risked even further rejection from the community. It took incredible courage for her to break those bonds of convention. She refused to accept her unhealed, rejected condition. She courageously did what she could to claim her right to healing, even if it went against the rules of the priests and against the norms of the community.

Jesus, by publicly acknowledging her touch, and proclaiming her great faith and her healing, healed not only her physical haemorrhage but also her place in the community.

This meditation is not only a meditation for women, despite the subject matter. All of us can relate to physical conditions or personal circumstances that have made us feel outcast, unclean. Many of us have been through experiences that have led others to see us that way. Many have been through divorce, loss of a pregnancy, physical illness, sexual abuse, physical disability. Some of us have experiences in our lives that have embedded shame deep into our souls. This meditation can be healing of such soul wounds.

Be prepared for this session to open up a lot of pain, but also the potential for great healing. For some, this may be the first time they have disclosed some of what they might say. Encourage people to be gentle with themselves, and remind them that they are free to share as much or as little as they choose.

GATHERING

Read the scripture aloud and then the reflection. Ask participants to reflect on the following questions:

- Where in your life have you felt unclean?
- Where have you felt invalidated, written off, rejected?
- Where have you felt that your very life blood was pouring out needlessly, in a way that drained life away, rather than giving life?

MEDITATION

Shut your eyes and let your body relax ... Let it sink into the chair or into the floor ... Let yourself be held up ... supported by the chair or floor ... You do not need to do the work of holding up your body ... You can let it be supported ... You can let go and relax ...

Begin to notice your breathing ... Breath is essential to living ... It was God's breath, we are told, that created all that is ... It has the power for cleansing and healing not only our physical system ... but also our emotional and spiritual lives ... Notice the breath as it begins at the tip of your nose ... Feel the cool air as it moves through your nostrils ... Follow it as it moves across the roof of your mouth ... Follow it as it goes down into your windpipe ... Follow it as it goes through your bronchial tubes into your lungs ... Notice where it goes into your lungs ... How deeply is the breath of life moving within you?

Gradually allow your breath to move more deeply into your being ... Let it open up space inside you ... space to meet the Holy ... space for you to BE ...

Gradually allow yourself to soften and flow with the breath ... Let your shoulders fall and relax as you breathe into the part of your lungs high up in your shoulders ... Let your tummy muscles relax and let go as you let the breath move deeply into your whole torso ... Notice what it feels like to be in your body-self as this happens ... Notice the feeling of letting go ... of relaxing ... of well-being ... of inner space for meeting the Holy ...

Pick one place (either the tip of the nose or a place in the lungs) in which to simply observe the breath as it passes ... in and out ... in and out ... Let yourself come to your sacred centre to the still place inside ...

Imagine yourself as the woman in the story who has been bleeding for twelve long years ... Imagine yourself in a small, hot community in Galilee ... Everyone knows who you are and what your problem is ... It had begun after you had given birth to your first child ... There is blood after all births, but this blood never stopped ... Imagine twelve years of agony ... twelve years of never being touched ... twelve years of being cast out by family ... by the whole community ... Twelve years of being mocked in the streets by young children who mouthed the cruel words to your face that their parents uttered in the silence of their homes ... Imagine the bleeding in your heart as this condition affects every relationship in your life ... No one can touch you without being considered unclean ... Your life blood is pouring out ... Your capacity for life in all its fullness if pouring out ...

Get in touch with the frustration of pouring out everything you had to get help ... You went to a doctor for help. He tried one thing, then another ... You went to another doctor, then another. They took your money, but none could heal you ... Your life blood ... pouring out. All your life savings, all your energy ... flowing out ... And all you got was scorn ... Get in touch with what it would be like to live such a life ...

You had been hearing about a Rabbi named Jesus who healed ... They said this man had cured the mother-in-law of one of his followers, Simon ... You've heard that Jesus had reached out his hand and actually touched a leper. He touched and cured an untouchable one ... Maybe he would also touch you ...

You feel that there is nothing left to lose ... Let rise within you the frustration and anger at being in this prison of uncleanness ... Get in touch with how tired you are of having your life blood pour out of you ... How sick you are of people looking away from you as if you are some contagious disease ... Feel the injustice of it all ... You are forced to bear the burden of a shame that you do not deserve ...You have done nothing wrong but bear a child ... and surely that is not wrong ... You are sick of being treated as unworthy, without dignity ... as a non-human being ... you are sick of being victimized ...

But there is also fear ... How will you find the courage to ask this man ... If you are caught, you could be stoned ... He is coming nearer ... Something in you drives you towards this last-ditch possibility of healing ... Imagine yourself leaving your home, keeping your face covered so people would not recognize you ... Thank goodness they were so preoccupied that they hardly paid attention to you ... You are watching him from afar trying to get your nerve up to go near ...

Then notice Jairus the leader of the synagogue go up to him and fall on his knees ... Jairus, one of the most powerful men in the town ... He is not afraid to beg ... His daughter is dying he says and he is beside himself with desperation ... Jesus is listening ... And he turns to go to Jairus' home ... Part of you is afraid that you have missed your chance ... After all a child of an important official needs him ... But there is another part or you that just pushes you forward ... almost in spite of yourself ... Your own longing and need for healing is driving you to act ... You think to yourself ... I don't need to bother him ... I can just touch his robe ... perhaps I would be healed ... There were fewer people behind him so you slip in that way as you move toward him ... Some people recognize you in the crowd ... but they step out of the way quickly and with disgust, so as not to become unclean ...

You use all your strength and every ounce of courage you can muster to get through the crowd to him ... He is moving away ... Quickly reach out your hand ... It is trembling with fear ... What are you afraid of? ... rejection? ... physical danger? ... perhaps healing itself? ... or what if it fails? ... What if it just turns out to be another disappointment? ...

Whatever the fear ... let the desire for healing ... the need for wholeness ... force you to touch the tassel of his cloak ... Feel the energy flow into you ... Feel the strength pour into your body ... Feel your whole body change as if it were waking up to life for the first time in years ... Feel the power to stand up straighter than you have stood in twelve long years ... Whatever has happened, you know that some things have changed ...

But then, just as you are about to fade back into the crowd, the Rabbi quickly turns around and faces your direction ... "Who touched my clothing?" he asks ... His disciples try to put him off, "Everyone is crowding in on you, how can you ask who touched you?" ... But he does not give up ... He seems to know that healing power has gone out from him ... He keeps looking around to see who had done it ... Feel your terror at having been found out ... you could be stoned for knowingly touching a Rabbi when you were unclean ... For twelve years the whole town had known of your situation ... You try to slip away quietly so no one would notice ... You don't need more rejection ...

But again he asks "Who touched me?" ... And this time his eyes meet yours and you feel that he must surely know who you are ... They draw you, these eyes ... You cannot hide ... Trembling you come in front of him and tell him the whole truth ... At first it feels horrible that you have to say it out loud in front of all these judging people ... But then you look deeply into his eyes that are filled with nothing but love and respect ... He is not looking at you the way the others do ... He is seeing right through to your soul ... And it is as if your can feel the love of God pour through those eyes into your wounded places ... And then you realize that he did not call you out to embarrass you or to blame you ... but to proclaim to the whole community that you are no longer unclean ...

Your body was healed when you touched his robe ... but you realize that your spirit was healed when he looked at you with love and compassion ... As you see his eyes, you even see some delight, as if you had just shared a very special, sacred moment together ... He is not ashamed to be touched by you ... He did not say that you were unclean ...The first person in twelve years who has not been ashamed ... Let yourself feel the burden of years of self-hatred flow out of you ...

He tells you that you are a daughter of God ... that you are filled with faith ... filled with faith ... Let those words penetrate deeply into your soul for they come from the heart of the loving, healing Christ ... "Your faith has cured you ... Go in peace and be free of this illness." ... "Be free" — Perhaps those words are more of a shock to your system than the blood stopping ... What affect do they have on the others? ...

Complete this part of the meditative journey in the way that brings closure for you ... Perhaps a thanksgiving to Christ ... perhaps some other ritual act ...

Now come away from the biblical story, and return to being yourself ...
How does this experience connect with your own life? ... What would it be
like for you to reach out to Christ for your own healing? ... What would it
be like to risk asking for what you need from God? ... What would it be like
for you to let the healing flow into you? ... What would it be like for you to
be told that your faith has healed you ... Be free ...

When you feel ready, bring your experience of healing with you as you
gradually make connection with this place ... with your body ... make some
gentle finger and toe movements ... Make some gentle circles with your
head ... Take some deep breaths — taking in the healing experience you
have had ... then when you are ready, gently open your eyes ... Look with
compassion at those who have shared this journey with you ... and allow
them to look into your eyes with the compassion of the healing Christ ...

SHARING

JOURNALLING/DRAWING

DEBRIEFING

Ask participants if they were able to get inside the experience of the bleeding
woman. Ask them to share what happened in their meditation, to the level they
feel able and comfortable:

- What connections were you able to make for your own life?
- Does this story make any sense in your life? Where do you connect?
- What was God doing for you in this meditation?
- What was God like for you?

CLOSURE

The Body Blessing (see Chapter 5) would work well with this meditation.

Because of the nature of this meditation, it can sometimes open up painful
wounds. Check with everyone to make sure that they are not leaving with unfinished business. If you feel that it is necessary, offer to meet with anyone who needs
to talk privately at another time.

10

HEALING FROM A DEEP DISAPPOINTMENT
THE BREAKFAST PARTY:
A MEDITATION FOR THE EASTER SEASON

INTRODUCTION
PREPARATION
- paper and pens/pencils/drawing materials
- photos of boats or fish, a candle, seashell, etc.
- flip chart (If you decide to use some of the questions that are part of the body of the meditation for the debriefing, choose those that you feel will be right for those in your own group. Put these on a flip chart to be used following the meditation.)

SCRIPTURE: JOHN 21:1–17

REFLECTION

This is another of the post-resurrection stories, and it appears only in John's Gospel. Here the appearance is in Galilee, although most of the other experiences in John's Gospel are in Jerusalem.

To prepare yourself to lead the meditation, imagine the seashore scene in Galilee. The disciples had returned to Galilee, after having witnessed the execution of the one that had captured their imaginations for these past few years. They had left everything to follow the vision he had not only preached but had lived out in all his actions. But now what had it all come to? Had they been fools to get caught up with this one who had led them down the garden path? Now he had left them hanging in mid-air, with no heart and no hope to carry on, but no way of turning back.

Some of the women had told them that they had seen the risen Christ. In fact they all thought they had seen him in the room where they had been huddled in fear when all the soldiers were looking for Galileans to arrest. But maybe that was just because they had so disparately wanted to see him. That happens in grief.

They thought he had told them to go back to Galilee. It had seemed real at the time. Besides, where else would they go? They waited — and waited and nothing happened. Finally Simon Peter, the most impetuous of the group, could stand it no longer. He was sick and tired of the useless waiting, the grieving, the kicking himself for having been taken in. "I'm going fishing!" he announces, "going back to what I know... at least doing something!"

GATHERING

a)   Remember a time when someone prepared food for you unexpectedly. Share what that meant to you and the feelings associated with it.

b)   Have you ever met someone again, unexpectedly, when you were sure you would never see them again? Reflect on that and share with others.

c)   Have you, or someone near you, ever experienced the presence of someone who has died? What was that like?

d)   Read the scripture, share the reflection above, and share where people find themselves in this story right now:

   •   Are you on the shore in grief and endless waiting, uncertain of how to go ahead or how to go backward?
   •   Are you out in the middle of the sea, trying to do what you used to do well, working but getting no results?
   •   Are you finding some new hope, some new way of doing things that is giving you real results from your effort?
   •   Are you being nourished by Christ, or by others in your life, so that you can carry on?

e)   As you think about Christ wanting to prepare a breakfast party to nourish and strengthen you, how do you react?

MEDITATION

Close your eyes ... Let yourself pay attention to what it feels like to be in this body-self that is you today ... right now ... Most of us go through whole days ... sometimes our whole lives ... without really paying attention to this body-self ... In Hebrew, the language Jesus knew, there was no such thing as disembodied spirit ... They spoke of the *nephesh* ... the body-soul ... the spirit/body ... Jesus talked about our bodies as temples of the Spirit ... What is it like for you to think of yourself in that way?

As you begin to pay attention to your body, do you notice places where tension is stored up?... where your muscles are in tight knots?... As you scan your body, from the top of your head to the bottom of your feet ... notice if there are tender places... sore spots ... and send compassion to these places in your body, thanking them for the hard work they are doing ... perhaps offering to pay more attention to what they are telling you in the future ... Become aware of your breathing, this life-sustaining process that goes on all of the time, even when we are unaware ... Notice if you are breathing with only a small part of your lungs, or whether you are taking the breath deeply into your whole being, down to the bottom of your lungs ... up to the tops of your shoulders ... Notice if your tummy moves in and out as you inhale and exhale ... the way a baby's does when it is breathing naturally ...

Notice where you are tightened up ... not fully open to the breath of life ... Let your body relax... let the tension flow out of your body through your feet ... Begin to allow your breath to move deeper into your being ... taking the breath deep down into your belly ... creating inner space ... Breathe in deeply the healing presence of the Spirit ... the goodness and grace of God ... Take it right into the core of your being ... As you breathe out, let the breath carry with it the poisons ... physical ... emotional ... spiritual ... that have built up in your system ... Breathe in possibility ... hope that the Spirit gives ... Let go of the stress and tensions that are stored in your body-self ... your emotional-self ... your spiritual-self ... Breathe in life energy ... The creating breath of God that was there from the beginning ... Breathe out whatever would block you from being fully present to this time...

Notice the inner space that is being prepared and opened up inside you ... space for the Sacred Presence to find room ... Space for the Holy One to be with you ... your own sacred space ... your own holy ground ... your sacred centre...

Get in touch with a time when you felt that all was lost ... everything for which you had put energy into in your life seemed gone ... expectations were not met ... Enter it only to the level that allows you to make a connection with the feelings that the disciples had as they waited by the Galilee shore ... Perhaps it was a time of loss ... of grief ... a time when your world was turned upside down ... The way ahead was not clear ...

Imagine yourself into the story of the disciples ... Hear this story moving through you as you become part of it in your imagination ... Imagine some of the feelings the disciples might have had as they waited on that Galilee shore ... Despair at losing their leader ... Still traumatized by the shock and horror of the crucifixion they had witnessed ... Questioning themselves about what it had all been about ... these last few years with Jesus ... Feeling the grief of losing a friend and leader ... Feeling also the grief of losing the purpose and direction for their lives ...

Imagine how unsure they must have felt about what to do next ... where to head with their lives ... Perhaps they were second guessing what they thought they had seen in Jerusalem when they had all been locked up in that God-forsaken room ... terrified of being arrested ... waiting for the soldiers to find them ... They thought they had seen Jesus ... At least it had seemed like Jesus was there ... But then grief does funny things to the mind ...

They thought they had been told to return to Galilee and he would come to them there ... But then where else would they go when everything was falling apart, except back to familiar territory? ... They were at least safer here than in Jerusalem ...where every Galilean was thought to be part of the resistance against Rome ...

And they waited... and waited and nothing happened ... There seemed no heart to go forward ...

Finally Simon Peter could stand it no longer ... He was sick and tired of the useless waiting ... the grieving ... the kicking himself for having been taken in ... "I'm going fishing!" he announced, "going back to what I know ... I have to do something ... anything." ...

In your mind's eye go with the disciples out into the boat on this moonlit night. ... When you are far enough from shore, imagine yourself casting the net with them ... exhausting yourself with back-breaking struggle...

All this hard work with no results ... endless amounts of energy expended ... but no results that lead anywhere ... Added to the grief is now the feeling of being drained ... exhausted from the seeming futility ...

Now imagine that you are looking to the shore ... to the edge ... to the place where the sea meets the earth ... In the very first light of dawn ... where day promises to break through the long dark night ... you notice movement ... Someone is there ... on the shore ... Perhaps someone else who could not sleep for troubled thoughts ...

This stranger ... this unknown one ... calls out telling you to try your net on the other side of the boat ... You have all been fishing all night ... You've had it ... What kind of reaction do you have to this person who thinks he knows more about where fish are than you? ...

But then you decide, there is nothing left to lose, and so you put down your nets on the other side ... One last try before giving up a lost cause ... Then comes the shock of your life! ... There is actually a huge school of fish right where the stranger told you to fish ... The weight of the net is almost more than all of you can drag in ...

Now take a moment to imagine that you are yourself again ... watching the scene at dawn ... Allow yourself space to reflect on the scene and its meaning in your life ...

What the disciples longed for was there ... right under their noses ... but they needed to approach it from a different point of view ... from the other side ... Be in touch with times in your life when what you needed was right there ... but you were unable to contact it until you were willing to see in a different way ... to act in a different way ... to come at things from the other side ...

Bring to mind times when you had to take a different approach in order to find the fruitfulness of all your work ... in order to connect with the meaning and the goodness that was there all the time ... The disciples had to pay attention to this one who came as a stranger ... unexpectedly ... even before they had any idea he was worth listening to ...

Who are the strangers in your life in whom you have recognized the Christ? ... Who might be the unexpected ones, the unknown ones, through whom God is trying to reach you? ... How open are you in your life to outsiders? ... to strangers? ... to a new way of seeing? ... Is there a part of you that is stranger, unknown, unacknowledged? ... Does this stranger in you have any wisdom to offer for your growth and healing? ...

The gifts of the sea that abounded convinced the shocked disciples that this stranger must be Jesus ... the one they had given up on ... the one who had died and abandoned them ... Peter is so shocked, that he puts on a heavy cloak to jump into the water ... without a thought about whether he'd drown in the weight of the thing ... The others show more sense ... staying in the boat ... making sure the fish they have caught come in with them ... Do you recognize anything of yourself in these two approaches to Christ? ...

Imagine yourself exhausted from a hard night's work, arriving at the shore ... smelling an open fire and the scent of fish barbecuing ... Christ has prepared breakfast for you ... bread and fish, lovingly prepared for you ... This is a Christ who longs to nurture you ... to care about the ordinary, physical needs you have ...

Can you imagine Christ inviting you to a breakfast party? ... What are the hungers in you that are crying out to be filled? ... What sort of food would you need from Christ? ... What sort of food would Christ long to give you? ... Are you able to receive it? ... Are you able to allow yourself to be cared for, to be given what you need by Christ?...

In the breaking of the bread, the disciples knew they were in the presence of the Holy ... What times do you know that you are in the presence of the Holy? ... Do you find Christ in the ordinary, concrete things in your life? ... in the strangers you meet? ... in the stranger inside yourself? ...

Ask God if there is any particular thing God would want to give you right now ... Take the time you need to do this ...

When you feel ready ... gradually get back in touch with your self that is here now in this physical place ... Make some gentle movements with your toes and fingers ... Get back in touch with your breathing ... Take some deep breaths ... Open your eyes gently when you are ready.

SHARING

JOURNALLING/DRAWING

DEBRIEFING

Invite participants to share as they feel comfortable any images or insights that happened for them during the experience. You might choose some of the questions that are in the meditation and invite the participants in twos or threes to share their response from the meditation.

CLOSURE

a)   Ask participants to call out one word or phrase of what God was doing in the group this evening.

b)   Sing: Stay With Us through the Night

THE BREAKFAST PARTY: A DAY-LONG RETREAT

PREPARATION

- handouts for participants to use during silent times: scripture, questions, other visuals, poems, etc.
- name tags
- worship centre

GATHERING

- Welcome participants, introduce the general theme, and ask each person to get in touch with a longing that is deep inside them as they come to this time of retreat (5 minutes).
- Use a), b) or c) of the gathering activities preceding the meditation, as participants introduce themselves and respond to the question (15 to 20 minutes).

MOVING DEEPER

- Use d) of the gathering activity, followed by journalling and reflection time (10 minutes).
- Sharing in the whole group, or in small groups if the group is too large (20 to 30 minutes).
- Do the meditation (30 minutes).

TIME OF SILENT REFLECTION

- Hand out the questions from the first part of the meditation for participants to reflect on in silence. I have used the questions from the sections relating to needing to approach things from a different perspective and recognizing the strangers in your life. I usually allow at least half an hour of silence, more if possible.
- Gather participants back to the circle if they have moved to other parts of the building for silence (I use a singing bowl or other bell).

SHARING

- Share as a whole group (30 minutes).
- Close the morning with a prayer that invites participants to say in one word or phrase what they have experienced God doing in this time.
- Sing: Stay With Us through the Night

BREAK

GATHERING

- In the afternoon, I would remind participants of the theme of the meditation very briefly just to get them back in touch. Singing "Stay With Us through the Night" again could serve the same purpose (5 minutes).

TIME OF SILENT REFLECTION

- Give participants the handout with scripture and the questions around the theme of breakfast party, and what God would want to give to nurture you.
- Allow silence of an hour. Some may wish to walk outside while they reflect, if this is convenient.

SHARING

- Gather back together for sharing reflections and comparing notes (45 minutes).

CLOSURE

- Sing "Stay With Us through the Night."
- End with Communion (15 minutes).

11

ON FORGIVENESS

INTRODUCTION

PREPARATION

- paper and pens/pencils/drawing materials
- David Augsberger's book *Caring Enough to Forgive/Caring Enough to Not Forgive*
- candle
- some stones
- any cards or sayings that relate to reconciliation and forgiveness

SCRIPTURE: MATTHEW 5:23–24

REFLECTION

Forgiveness is a difficult issue for Christians, since many of us feel that we are required to offer forgiveness in all circumstances and are inadequate spiritually if we find this impossible. We take forgiveness too lightly.

I have met abused women who carry a burden of guilt and inadequacy because, try as they may, they could not forgive the abuser who showed absolutely no remorse or took any responsibility for the pain caused. Some had consulted other ministers or priests and been told that they should forgive, understand, and live with the abuse. To add insult to injury, they were sometimes told that they should try to discover what they were doing that caused it to happen. I find this an obscenity.

Forgiveness, which I understand to mean restoration of right relationship, cannot happen in cases where one party is expected to do all the forgiving and there is no remorse, repentance, or owning of responsibility on the part of the abuser. Until there is justice, it is very difficult to restore right relationship and have reconciliation.

Acceptance of reality, healing, honouring the experience but refusing to allow it to define your future, letting go of the hurt and releasing the power of the other to hold you hostage: these are possible in such a one-way situation. Forgiveness, the restoration of relationship, may not be there unless the abuser is willing to take responsibility and to show by changed behaviour that the words have meaning.

On the other hand, I have met people who nurse old hurts and are not willing to let them go even though they have long out-lived their usefulness. It is as if these wounds have become old friends that keep life stuck. It is possible for a person to get locked into a victim role and become unable to move on and claim life in all its fullness. It is sometimes frightening to claim healing and one's own power.

I have learned a great deal about this from Aboriginal peoples. In 1986, The United Church of Canada, of which I am a minister, apologized to Aboriginal peoples within our church community for the destruction of their culture and spirituality that occurred in bringing the gospel of Christ. It was two years later that the All-Native Circle Conference responded with an acknowledgement of the apology, not an acceptance. In other words, they said that they had heard what we said as a church; but words did not mean that an apology was real. It would become real as it was lived out in changed behaviour and in renewed relationship. If nothing changed, the apology had little power. If there truly was repentance, then the apology would become a new beginning of restored relationship and forgiveness would be enacted as that happened.

I have found the work of David Augsburger, a Mennonite pastor and psychotherapist very helpful in the issue of forgiveness. Augsburger focuses on forgiveness being about restoration of right relationship between two people. Forgiveness is a process not a single act. When two people desire to move towards right relationship by recognizing wrong and hurt, and by letting go of unjust demands, the process of forgiveness can begin. It may take a long period of working out the issues involved. It would result in changed behaviour, in a new beginning, in restoration of respect for one another.

Augsburger takes Jesus as a model for his expression of anger and forgiveness. Jesus behaved in different ways in different circumstances. He was comfortable in expressing anger, and in choosing not to express it under certain circumstances. He forgave, and he also turned forgiveness over to God, as he did on the cross.

Augsburger suggests that we should care enough to forgive whenever possible, but that we should care enough to not forgive when forgiveness is offered cheaply; when it is one-way; when hurt is not recognized; when there is no genuine repentance. In such cases the best one can do is to keep an open heart and mind to the possibility of forgiveness, and to do the work that is possible within one's own soul to come to terms with and let go of the control the hurt has on your life. Sometimes this involves forgiving oneself. Often we find others easier to forgive than ourselves.

This meditation is one that can be repeated many times, when one has identified that it is time to let go of a particular person or issue. It is very important that the leader avoid making anyone feel guilty for not being at a point of readiness to forgive someone, particularly when there are unresolved circumstances. For some, it is good news that there are times when one needs to honour one's pain and have it witnessed. To be rushed too quickly into forgiveness seals off the wound before it has even begun to have a chance to heal. There are other times, when it really is time to let go of a wound, to let go of a hurt. The hurt has been honoured, given its space to grieve and the time has come to begin the process of letting go and releasing both yourself, and the other to the life of the Spirit.

GATHERING

a) Can you remember a time in your life when you have been forgiven for something (large or small)? What did that feel like? Share with the group, or with one other person, depending upon your group.

b) Where did you learn what you know about forgiveness? What did you learn?

c) Read the scripture slowly, noting that Jesus sees a connection between our relationships with others and our relationship with God. Ask participants to share their feelings about this.

d) Share some of the approach from the reflection, or if you are able to have one or more copies of David Augsburger's book available, allow people to look at the table of contents for both halves of the book. One half is *Caring Enough to Forgive*. When you turn the book over, upside-down, the other title is *Caring Enough to Not Forgive*. This will often come as a great surprise to people.

e) Make a list of people from whom you feel alienated. The person may be alive or dead. It may be someone you are able to speak with, or someone you will never actually be able to contact. Prayerfully choose one of these people whom you feel called to work on right now. It may not be the most difficult person on your list. It may not be even someone you expected to be called to work on, but allow the Spirit to offer you leading on which person you might want to work on.

MEDITATION

Close your eyes ... Let yourself pay attention to what it feels like to be in this body-self that is you today ... right now ... Most of us go through whole days ... sometimes our whole lives ... without really paying attention to this body-self ... In Hebrew, the language Jesus knew, there was no such thing as disembodied spirit ... They spoke of the *nephesh* ... the body-soul ... the spirit/body ... Jesus talked about our bodies as temples of the Spirit.

As you begin to pay attention to your body, do you notice places where tension is stored up? ... where your muscles are in tight knots? ... As you scan your body, from the top of your head to the bottom of your feet ... notice if there are tender places... sore spots ... and send compassion to these places in your body, thanking them for the hard work they are doing ... perhaps offering to pay more attention to what they are telling you in the future ... Become aware of your breathing, this life-sustaining process that goes on all of the time, even when we are unaware ... Notice if you are breathing with only a small part of your lungs, or whether you are taking the breath deeply into your whole being, down to the bottom of your lungs ... up to the tops of your shoulders ... Notice if your tummy moves in and out as you inhale and as you exhale... the way a baby's does when it is breathing naturally ...

Notice where you are tightened up ... not fully open to the breath of life ... Let your body relax ... let the tension flow out of your body through your feet. ... Begin to allow your breath to move deeper into your being ... taking the breath deep down into your belly ... creating inner space ... Breathe in deeply the healing presence of the Spirit ... the goodness and grace of God ... Take it right into the core of your being ... As you breathe out, let the breath carry with it the poisons ... physical ... emotional ... spiritual ... that have built up in your system ... Breathe in possibility ... hope that the Spirit gives ... Let go of the stress and tensions that are stored in your body-self ... your emotional-self ... your spiritual-self ... Breathe in life energy ... The creating breath of God that was there from the beginning ... Breathe out whatever would block you from being fully present to this time ...

Again notice your body ... If there continue to be tense places, imagine this healing breath moving directly to those spots ... unknotting the tension ... letting go ... letting be ... letting open ... letting unlock ... Know that you are in a safe place ... that this is a place where it is safe to be ... Notice the inner space that is being prepared and opened up inside you ... space for the Sacred Presence to find room ... Space for the Holy One to be with you ... Your own sacred space ... your own holy ground ... Your own sacred centre where you meet the Holy ...

Imagine that you are in a very sacred place ... It is a special place for encountering the Holy ... notice what it looks like ... the colours ... the structures the smells ... the sounds ... Are there other people there? ... What are they doing? ... Know that you are very near the Holy ... Know that this is a safe and sacred place filled with love and beauty ... Know that you are here because you are longing to be nearer to God ... Longing to feel deeply connected to the Spirit ...

Become aware of the gift that you are bringing as an offering to this Holy Presence ... Notice what it is ... While you are standing prepared to offer it notice if there is anyone who comes to mind against whom you feel resentment or who feels resentment against you ... In the presence of the Sacred Source of unconditional love become aware of someone with whom you do not feel at peace, someone with whom you feel out of right relationship ... It may not be the most painful relationship ... or it may not be the most difficult person for you to deal with ... It may be you who have done wrong, or it may be the other who has hurt you ... Allow the Spirit to lead and to choose ...

When you have identified the person with whom you have unfinished business, imagine your highest-self, your sacred-self encountering the highest-self of the other ... Know that this is a safe place. You can ask for help from anyone you need to be with you ... and you can be as far away from this person as you need to be to feel safe ...

Speak to this person as you are able at this time ... Imagine the other person responding to what you have said ... Listen carefully ... Dialogue back and forth with the person for as long as the dialogue can continue ... You may only be able to say one sentence ... or you may speak for a long time ... Go as far as is possible in the dialogue today ... As you are finishing ... ask the person ... Is there some wisdom or learning or growth for your own development that they can offer you? ... Receive whatever is offered ... Once you have gone as far as you are able to go at this time ... invite God to bless that person as well as yourself ...

If you reach a point of resolution with the person ... surround that person with love and release them to God's care ... You might want to imagine surrounding them with the Light of Christ ... the Light of Love ... Draw back into yourself the energy that has been pouring out ... draining you and keeping you connected even in your estrangement ... You might want to image that as drawing back chords of connection that have been tying you to the other ... Feel the freedom and spiritual energy that return to you to give you power ...

When you feel ready, return to the sacred place where you were bringing your gift when you began this dialogue ... Approach this place knowing that you have done what is possible at this time ... If there is someone else with whom you have unfinished business who comes to mind while you are there ... you might wish to repeat the process of dialogue with another ...

As you return to the sacred place when you are finished your work for today ... experience the love that pours from that place ... surrounding you ... pouring through you ... As you return to the altar you discover that the Holy has left a gift for you ... What is it? ... What does it feel like to receive this gift? ...

Take the time to make whatever closure is appropriate for you ... then move out of this sacred place ... bringing with you the wisdom and learning you have received, and the gift the Holy One gave to you ... Gradually become aware of yourself as you are sitting (or lying) ... Notice your breathing ... make some gentle movements with your fingers and toes and head ... When you are ready, open your eyes.

SUPPLEMENTARY MATERIAL

If space allows, I often invite people to an embodied meditation on this theme. First of all I lead the meditation, and then I invite them to find a personal space.

Imagine that you are constructing an altar of stones and bringing an offering to it ... Let the spirit suggest what the offering is ... As you bring the offering, notice if there is a person or an issue blocking you. Then, either using two chairs facing each other, or using two spots on the floor, standing or sitting, imagine yourself in dialogue with the issue or the person. Once you have gone as far as you can go with the conversation, return to the altar and notice that God has left a gift there for you. Notice what the gift is then make a closure that feels right for you.

SHARING

JOURNALLING/DRAWING

Participants may wish to draw the gift received, or to write down key insights, words or ideas that they want to keep with them in the next week.

DEBRIEFING

Allow participants to share what happened for them in the meditation. Ask participants if there is any action they wish to take in the next while as a result of their meditation. If there is, some may wish to share that.

CLOSURE

Choose one from Chapter 5.

———•◦•———

This meditation may stir up issues that participants may wish to speak privately with you about. Make sure that you notice anyone who does not speak, and make contact. As they leave, you might check with each person to see how they feel.

PART III

Meditations for Growth and Strength

12

THE PARABLE OF THE SOWER
AND THE SEED

INTRODUCTION

PREPARATION
- paper and pens/pencils/drawing materials
- bowl of seeds along with some stones and twigs
- a plant that has grown in difficult conditions

SCRIPTURE: MATTHEW 13:1–9, MARK 4:1–9

REFLECTION

Jesus used different aspects and stages of plant life, from the time of sowing the seed to the time of growth and harvesting, to talk to us about ourselves and the nature of spiritual growth. He spoke of God's reign as a small seed that, once planted, became a great tree. He spoke of growth that takes place in secret. He also spoke of us as the earth that receives the seed. In fact in this parable, he suggests we are several kinds of earth, some that can receive and nurture the seed, and others that cannot.

This is a meditation that continues to work in a person after it happens. It is a useful one to do often.

MEDITATION

Shut your eyes and let your body relax ... Let it sink into the chair or into the floor ... Let yourself be held up ... supported by the chair or floor ... You

do not need to do the work of holding up your body ... You can let it be
supported ... You can let go and relax ...

Begin to notice your breathing ... Breath is essential to living ... It was God's
breath, we are told, that created all that is ... It has the power for cleansing
and healing not only our physical system ... but also our emotional and
spiritual lives ... Notice the breath as it begins at the tip of your nose ... Feel
the cool air as it moves through your nostrils ... Follow it as it moves across
the roof of your mouth ... Follow it as it goes down into your windpipe ...
Follow it as it goes through your bronchial tubes into your lungs ... Notice
where it goes into your lungs ... How deeply is the breath of life moving
within you? ...

Gradually allow your breath to move more deeply into your being ... Let it
open up space inside you ... space to meet the Holy ... space for you to BE ...

Gradually allow yourself to soften and flow with the breath ... Let your
shoulders fall and relax as you breathe into the part of your lungs high up
in your shoulders ... Let your tummy muscles relax and let go as you let the
breath move deeply into your whole torso ... Notice what it feels like to be
in your body-self as this happens ... Notice the feeling of letting go ... of
relaxing ... of well-being ... of inner space for meeting the Holy ...

Pick one place (either the tip of the nose or a place in the lungs) in which to
simply observe the breath as it passes ... in and out ... in and out ... Let
yourself come to your sacred centre to the still place inside ...

Visualize a field that is out-of-doors ... As you look at the field, you become
aware that it is made up of many different parts ... Notice a footpath that is
hard and trodden down by many who have passed that way ... See how the
grass that has tried to grow in this place has found it impossible to grow
beyond scraggy stubble ... Part of the field is overgrown with weeds and
thorn trees ... Part of the field is a rock pile ... a place where stones that had
been in the way were piled up on rocks that were already there ... Part of the
field has been well dug ... well prepared for gardening ... There has been the

right amount of mulch and nutrient dug in ... The weeds and rocks have been removed ... Look at this whole field very intently in your mind's eye ...

Notice the birds that fly in the area ... Get a sense of the smells and sounds in this field ... Now let yourself become this piece of ground ... this field with many types of earth ... Experience the ground of your self ... Experience it being made up of many different parts ...

Experience the footpath or the wayside in yourself ... the part of yourself that has become hardened and beaten down ... the part of yourself that has become worn. The birds took the seed from the footpath in the story Jesus told ... What happens to insights or thoughts that fall on your footpath? ... Be in touch with something in your life that has been picked up and taken away before it has had a chance to grow ... Notice your feelings about that ...

Experience the shallow or rocky ground of your self ... Experience what happens to the seeds of new life that fall on your shallow, rocky ground ... Watch a seed fall on this part of your ground ... Watch it begin to sprout up quickly ... then watch it die as it has not been deeply rooted ... as it does not have a root system capable of sustaining growth ... Allow it to remind you of something that has withered in your life because it was not securely rooted ... Notice the feelings that arise ...

Experience the weedy, tangled part of yourself ... the part that has been give no attention and is showing the results of that lack of care ... Experience what happens to opportunities for growth and life that fall on this tangled part of your self ... Let yourself be reminded of things in your life that have been choked out by other interests and activities ... Notice the feelings that arise ...

Experience the dark, rich, well-dug part of yourself ... the part that has been tended ... the part that has been nurtured and well watered ... What happens to seeds of new life that fall on this part of your self? ... Be in touch with what in your life has grown well and has been given space and care ... Notice the fruit that it gives ... What in your life has born great fruit? ...

Take some time to reflect on yourself as this varied field of earth ... Where is it possible for seeds of growth to fall and for new growth to take root in you? ... What are the beaten-down places in your life that prevent growth? ... What part of yourself is too busy ... too overgrown for anything new to find space? ... What part of yourself has bursts of enthusiasm about new life, but when resistance from inside or outside is met, will not let the roots grow properly? ... What parts of yourself are so confused and chaotic that nothing can grow? ... What are the stones of resistance in you? ... the thorn trees and weeds that block growth? ... Where is the rich well-prepared space for growth ...

Are there places that you need to consciously work on preparing for growth? ... Is there clearing out that needs to happen? ... Is there attention and care that needs to be given to the earth that you are, so that you can nurture life and growth? ... How might you begin? ...

Gradually draw yourself back to this space and to your body-self ... Take the breath of life deep into your being ... Allow it to nurture the growth that is taking place in you in this meditation ... Reconnect with your body-self, as it is sitting (or lying down) ... Open your eyes when you feel ready ...

SHARING
JOURNALLING/DRAWING

DEBRIEFING
Ask participants to share what happened for them in the meditation:
- What do you feel called to do in your own life about the soil that is your self?
- Where might you begin?
- What resistance might you meet to doing this?
- What help do you need to do this?

CLOSURE
Choose one from Chapter 5.

13

THE PARABLE OF THE GROWING SEED

INTRODUCTION

PREPARATION
- paper and pens/pencils/drawing materials
- bowl of seeds
- a newly sprouting seed in a see-through container

SCRIPTURE: MARK 4:26–29
Other scriptures using seed imagery are the parable of the mustard seed, Matthew 13:31–32, Mark 4:30–32, Luke 13:18–19; and the Parable of the Sower and the Seed Mark 4:1–9, Matthew 13:1–9.

REFLECTION

All growth begins with recognition of need. One could almost say of the seed that it must recognize its poverty as a seed before it can desire to grow into a plant. Without this "need" the seed could not die to being a seed and risk sending out tender vulnerable shoots into the darkness of the soil. The journey to growth, once begun, has no turning back. The safe shell of the seed disintegrates; it dies. The pull towards growth must be sufficiently strong to carry the shoot forward in the process until it breaks through the ground and becomes a plant.

The seed has locked up inside itself some vision of what is possible for it to become. And it also has the will to grow inherent in it, and the knowledge that such growth is possible, and is indeed the fulfilment of its meaning. These have been gifted by the Creator from the beginning.

Jesus put people in touch with the potential within them for growth and transformation. He helped people develop the trust necessary that God's Spirit was active as power for growth and transformation right in their very midst.

He helped those who felt they had no possibility to grow because they had no value or purpose. These he lifted up and called out their strength and power. He challenged those who were closed to growth because they thought they already knew all they needed to know. These he opened up with stories that invited transformation.

GATHERING

a) Where do you have a sense of a quality that is growing in you at this time of your life?

b) If you imagine the process of a plant's growth, and you think about your own growth, or some particular aspect of it, what phase of the process do you identify with?

c) If you were to choose one quality that is not very well developed in you, but that you would like to have grow in your life, what would that be? Participants might appreciate a chance to journal about this before the meditation begins.

MEDITATION

Shut your eyes and let your body relax ... Let it sink into the chair or into the floor ... Let yourself be held up ... supported by the chair or floor ... You do not need to do the work of holding up your body ... You can let it be supported ... You can let go and relax ...

Begin to notice your breathing ... Breath is essential to living ... It was God's breath, we are told, that created all that is ... It has the power for cleansing and healing not only our physical system ... but also our emotional and spiritual lives ... Notice the breath as it begins at the tip of your nose ... Feel the cool air as it moves through your nostrils ... Follow it as it moves across the roof of your mouth ... Follow it as it goes down into your windpipe ... Follow it as it goes through your bronchial tubes into your lungs ... Notice where it goes into your lungs ... How deeply is the breath of life moving within you? ...

Gradually allow your breath to move more deeply into your being ... Let it open up space inside you ... space to meet the Holy ... space for you to BE ...

Gradually allow yourself to soften and flow with the breath ... Let your shoulders fall and relax as you breathe into the part of your lungs high up in your shoulders ... Let your tummy muscles relax and let go as you let the breath move deeply into your whole torso ... Notice what it feels like to be in your body-self as this happens ... Notice the feeling of letting go ... of relaxing ... of well-being ... of inner space for meeting the Holy ...

Pick one place (either the tip of the nose or a place in the lungs) in which to simply observe the breath as it passes ... in and out ... in and out ... Let yourself come to your sacred centre to the still place inside ...

Imagine you are in an area that would be a good place to plant a seed so that it would grow well ... Be in touch with the setting in which you find yourself ... Notice the colours of the scene ... Notice what is around you ... Are you indoors or outdoors? ... What sort of day is it? ... Are there any scents in the air? ... Any sounds? ...

Now imagine yourself as a seed that is about to be put into the ground ... Experience being the seed ... Experience the colour and shape you are ... Experience the smallness ... Experience the hardness of the shell of protection around you ... Experience the safe-ness of being a seed ...

Allow yourself to be put into the earth ... What is the earth like where you are planted? ... You are still the seed ... but now you are planted in the earth ... and as the sun warms you and the rain softens your shell ... experience a force or a power working in you ... causing something in you to vibrate ... calling out the desire in you to move out beyond the confines of your shell ...

Feel the draw to be more ... Feel the force of creation working in you ... Notice your response ... Do you feel some resistance to the change? ... some fear of the unknown? ... Is there part of you that wants to hang on to the familiar? ... to your seed-ness? ...

Now allow the desire for growth, and the call to fulfilment, work within you until it gradually becomes stronger than your fear of change ... Experience the force of creation calling you forth in a way that you become ready to respond ... Feel the warmth of the sun beckoning to you ... Feel the gentle rain softening your seed-shell ... Feel the first new roots reaching down into the soil ... pushing deeper and deeper into the earth ... giving you a base for growth ... giving you a source of nourishment for on-going growth ...

Then experience the tiny shoot pushing up through the darkness of the soil ... Are there obstacles in the way? ... stones or rocks that must be gone around? ... Feel the pull to light and warmth more strongly now as it beckons you onward ... Allow yourself to break through the soil to the light ... Experience the excitement of breaking out into the light ... the newness of the experience of space and air and light ... Experience as deeply as you can this entry into a whole new dimension ... Feel the emotions that rise up in you as you are on your way to becoming what you were meant to be ...

Watch yourself grow ... as the plant you are becoming gets stronger and stronger ... more and more sure of itself ... As it discovers more and more of what had been lying dormant in itself when it was seed ... Allow yourself to draw the nurture and strength you need ... from the earth ... from the rain ... from the sun ... from the air ...

How do you feel about what you are becoming? ... Invite the Spirit to offer you insights about what has happened for your life ... How does the Spirit feel about the growth taking place in you?...

Gradually allow yourself to return to see the place where you were planted ... to reconnect with your body-self ... to find your breath and the soles of your feet ... to make gentle stretching movements with your toes and fingers and neck ... and gently draw yourself back to the group and to open your eyes ...

SHARING

Journalling/Drawing

Debriefing

Invite participants to share as they feel comfortable, their experience of the meditation:

- How does this meditation connect with what is happening in your life?
- What seed of growth is being planted in you at this time in your life?

CLOSURE

After debriefing, it might be good to invite participants to take one of the seeds in the bowl, and to tell the group what seed of growth they feel is being planted in them at this time. This seed can then be taken home as a visible reminder of this promise and possibility.

14

SPACE FOR GROWTH

INTRODUCTION

PREPARATION
- paper and pens/pencils/drawing materials
- cloth
- candle
- open Bible
- images that evoke fullness and emptiness (Perhaps a bowl full to overflowing with something like potpourri and another bowl completely empty.)

SCRIPTURE
The theme of this meditation is related to many scriptures including:
- Matthew 5:1–8 or Luke 6:20–22 (The Beatitudes)
- John 3:1–9 (Nicodemus visits Jesus by night)
- Luke 18:18–25 (The rich young ruler)

REFLECTION
This meditation is not specifically linked with any one scripture, but is quite central to Jesus' teaching that those who hunger for spiritual growth are those who will have it; not those who are already filled up with physical, spiritual, emotional accumulation. Without space, and an acknowledgement of inner poverty, there is not much room for growth to take place.

One scripture I have used with this theme is the Beatitudes, Matthew 5:1–8 or Luke 6:20–22. It could be used with either the story of the rich young ruler or of Nicodemus' visit to Jesus by night. In both cases, it was difficult for them to find space in their reality systems for the radical teaching of Jesus. They might have hoped that they need not give up too much of what they already possessed, but could just "add on" Jesus' truth. But Jesus' teaching required a complete reorienting of reality systems.

The meditation also fits with the theme reinforced in both Hebrew and Christian scripture: that there are those whose hearts are hardened and cannot see or hear the truth. Throughout Jesus' life it was in the unexpected places, the places where emptiness was known, that new life could come. Jesus said that he came for those who knew they were estranged or disconnected from God and from themselves, not for those who were certain of their wellness and out of touch with their empty hurting places.

The house is an archetypal symbol for the self. Each level represents some part of the person's being. This meditation allows us to experience both our fullness and our emptiness.

GATHERING

a)   Ask participants to think about the favourite room in their home and to share why this is so.

b)   Ask participants to identify places in their lives that feel full. How do they feel about the "fullness" in their lives? Some may feel content and satisfied with parts of their lives that are experiencing God's fullness. Others may feel overwhelmed by schedules and demands that allow no space for themselves and pull them in many directions.

c)   Introduce the scripture you have chosen with some of the material from the reflection. As those gathered begin to meditate they need to know that the theme of the meditation is on fullness and emptiness.

MEDITATION

Shut your eyes and let your body relax ... Let it sink into the chair or into the floor ... Let yourself be held up ... supported by the chair or floor ... You do not need to do the work of holding up your body ... You can let it be supported ... You can let go and relax ...

Begin to notice your breathing ... Breath is essential to living ... It was God's breath, we are told, that created all that is ... It has the power for cleansing and healing not only our physical system ... but also our emotional and spiritual lives ... Notice the breath as it begins at the tip of your nose ... Feel the cool air as it moves through your nostrils ... Follow it as it moves across the roof of your mouth ... Follow it as it goes down into your windpipe ... Follow it as it goes through your bronchial tubes into your lungs ... Notice where it goes into your lungs ... How deeply is the breath of life moving within you?

Gradually allow your breath to move more deeply into your being ... Let it open up space inside you ...space to meet the Holy ...space for you to BE ...

Gradually allow yourself to soften and flow with the breath ... Let your shoulders fall and relax as you breathe into the part of your lungs high up in your shoulders ... Let your tummy muscles relax and let go as you let the breath move deeply into your whole torso ... Notice what it feels like to be in your body-self as this happens ... Notice the feeling of letting go ... of relaxing ... of well-being ... of inner space for meeting the Holy ...

Pick one place (either the tip of the nose or a place in the lungs) in which to simply observe the breath as it passes ... in and out ... in and out ... Let yourself come to your sacred centre to the still place inside ...

Visualize yourself standing outside a middle-eastern-style house that has two stories and a flat roof and is white-washed ... There are two sides to this house and the door opens in the middle to both halves ... Get a sense of the house ... of its size ... of the location around it ...

Notice if it is well kept, or needs work ... Is it day or night? ... Are the lights on or off? ... How do you feel about this house as you look at it from the outside before you enter it? ... In your mind's eye walk up to the door of this house ... open the door ... and walk in ... turn to the right ...

Explore the rooms on the bottom floor ... They are full of possessions ... your own possessions ... Experience your satisfaction and self-assurance and confidence as you are aware of yourself having these possessions ... Move through the rooms, just being aware of the fullness of your life in practical material matters ... Notice the feelings that arise as you experience your material possessions ...

Now go up a flight of stairs to the second level and experience here the fullness of your own mental possessions ... the knowledge and skill that you have ... the knowledge that has come from the experiences of your life ... your intellectual knowledge ... Experience as fully as you can the completeness of your knowing as it now exists ... And sense how this knowing, along with your material possessions, helps to define your sense of your own identity ... How do you feel as you are aware of all of this knowledge you possess? ...

There is also a spiritual place in this side of the house ... It may be only a corner of a room ... Experience this place that contains your spiritual beliefs and practices ... the principles that make your life seem right ... the principles that you live by ... How do you feel about your spiritual knowing as you experience this side of the house? ... Is it confining or demanding? ... Or does it feel open and free? ...

Now go back to the front door of this house ... Just before you leave this side of the house, experience the feeling you get from this entire side of the house ... Does it feel complete in itself? ... Do you experience its lack of space? ... Do you feel there is room for anything new to enter into this part of the house? ... Do you feel the longing for more, or are you content with this side of the house just the way it is? ... If you are content with the house as it is, leave the meditation now by shutting the door and returning to an awareness of your body ...

If you have experienced any lack of space in this half of the house, or any sense of being confined in it, enter the left side of the house ... On the ground floor you find only one room and it is completely empty ... Experience its barrenness ... the shock of its barrenness ... Experience its poverty ... Experience the feelings of being without possessions ... Experience the barrenness in yourself ... the part of yourself you do not often inhabit ... Now move to one of the windows and look out ... Notice the beauty of nature that is visible to you ... the earth ... the plants and trees that are near at hand ... Notice what is at a distance ... Notice the sky, and its reflections of light ... Notice any clouds ... Open yourself to what you can see outside, knowing that there is much to feed upon ... Notice people passing by the window ... passing in the distance ... Experience deep compassion for them as you have space to be open to them ... as you experience them without the barrier of your possessions and the self-confidence they give you ... Experience your sensitivity and your vulnerability as you watch people passing ... and the deep caring that flows from your own sense of need ...

Now experience your spiritual needs ... as you are able to feel them in this exposed place ... Allow yourself to go upstairs to a room above and experience the emptiness of your mind and your knowing ... your own not-knowing ... In that place allow your desire to be filled with real truth ... and real wisdom to arise in you ...

Notice a ladder in the corner of the room that leads to the roof ... and as you climb up that ladder experience your own deepest heart's desire to know God ... As you come out of your sense of need ... and out of your desire and longing for truth and connection with the Holy ... allow yourself to encounter what you need ... Allow yourself to vision what you most need ... Allow the Spirit to meet you in your needs ... Ask for what you need, as you are able ... How is your need, and your longing received? ... Does the Spirit offer you anything? ... Take whatever time you need in this encounter with the Holy ... making whatever closure is appropriate for you as you leave that place... Climb down the ladder ... and return to the front door ...

At the front door, pause for a moment to reflect on what you have experienced and what you have learned ... As you look at both sides of the house, which side will you want others to see? ... Which side will you want to return to for further spiritual growth? ... Then come out of the house and shut the door and return slowly to this place ... Gradually get in touch with the body ... Take some deep breaths ... Make some gentle movements with your toes and fingers ... some circles with your head ... Become aware of your body as it touches the chair ... the floor ... and open your eyes when you feel ready.

SHARING

JOURNALLING/DRAWING

DEBRIEFING

Invite participants to share, as they wish, their experience of the meditation:

- How did you feel about the two different sides of your house?
- Where did you feel invited to spend more time?
- Did you go into the second, empty side of the house?
- If you did, what was your experience of the Holy?
- What needs did you feel rise up in you?
- Did you receive anything?

CLOSURE

Ask participants to call out, in one word or phrase, what God was doing in this meditation time for them. Close with a prayer that gathers all of this together, then pass the peace of Christ (always being sensitive to the preference of some persons not be touched).

MEDITATION

15

SEEKING AND ASKING

INTRODUCTION

PREPARATION

- paper and pens/pencils/drawing materials
- a cloth
- candle
- open Bible
- visual cues about seeking and finding, asking and receiving, knocking and having the door opened

SCRIPTURE: MATTHEW 7:7–11, LUKE 11:5–13

REFLECTION

The spiritual journey is a delicate balance between what we can and ought to do ourselves in order to grow spiritually and emotionally and what we need to let go of to trust in a Spirit greater than ourselves. There is an active role for us in letting go of what we have outgrown and no longer need, so that we can create space for the new. But the journey also involves the need to seek and trust a power greater than ourselves. The Sacred's love and power is greater than our own, and we need to open ourselves to it in order to keep growing spiritually. It will guide us to our higher selves, and into deeper wisdom and truth about ourselves and our path.

We are blocked on the journey when we are so full that there is not any room for the new. We are also blocked when we are unaware of our needs, or when we are afraid to trust and to ask.

The aim of this meditation is to awaken the seeking, asking part of us. Sometimes when we think we are asking for one thing, our unconscious is asking for something else. Bernie Siegal in his books on cancer recovery, has discovered that, often, people say they have a desire for healing, but their drawings, meditations, and dreams betray a very different reality operating in the unconscious.

We have many levels of asking and seeking; we need to be aware of these different levels. Until we become aware of ourselves as seeking, asking, desiring, needing selves, our forms of asking may contradict each other. As we become aware, we may discover some forms of asking that contradict our spiritual growth. Part of us wants to grow; another part still longs for security and protection from change. Part of us wants to know truth; another part is afraid of what it will find out. Part of us wants to do what is needed to heal past wounds and memories; another part clings to a familiar pattern that we hold in place, even though we complain about it and profess our hatred of it. Part of us wants to be all that God has created us to be; another part prefers to hide behind powerlessness and excuses to stay in the same place.

As we clarify our seeking, we can begin to sort out and evaluate the kinds of asking that are within us. There are times and seasons for different kinds of asking, and part of wisdom is knowing how to ask and what to ask for at any particular time.

MEDITATION

Shut your eyes ... let yourself begin to connect with this body-self that you are ... this holy temple ... Many of us spend our whole lives disconnected from our body-self ... We take our body for granted ... We do not recognize it as created in God's image ... as a source of wisdom and profound knowing ... Ask your body to teach you its wisdom as your relax ... as you tell your mind that it doesn't need to help you for the next while ... that it is good for you to relax and just be for the next little while ... Tell your mind that it can take a rest ... that you appreciate that it is trying to help, but that just for now you want to be fully present to your body-self ... and to its wisdom ... As you begin to pay attention to your body, do you notice places where tension is stored up? ... where your muscles are in tight knots? ... As you scan your body, from the top of your head to the bottom of your feet ... notice if there are tender places ... sore spots ... and send compassion to these places in your body, thanking them for the hard work they are doing ... perhaps offering to pay more attention to what they are telling you in the future... Befriend the places of pain in your body ...

Become aware of your breathing ... of the life-sustaining breath that goes on all of the time ... even when we are unaware ... Notice if you are breathing with only a small part of your lungs, or whether you are taking the breath deeply into your whole being ... down to the bottom of your lungs ... Breathe with your whole torso ... your whole body... Take the breath of life up to the tops of your shoulders ... a place where many of us store stress and the heavy loads we are carrying ... Notice if your tummy moves in and out as you inhale and exhale ... the way a baby's does when it is breathing naturally ...

Notice where you are tightened up ... not fully open to the breath of life ... Let your body relax ... let the tension flow out of your body through your feet ... Begin to allow your breath to move deeper into your being ... taking the breath deep down into your belly ... creating inner space ... Breathe in deeply the healing presence of the Spirit ... the goodness and grace of God ... Take it right into your centre ... With each breath out, allow the breath to carry away the toxins that have built up ... the physical poisons that need to be cleansed ... Let it also carry out the emotional poisons that have been stored in your body ... the pains and angers that need to be let go ... Let the healing breath gently caress the wounded places ... let the life-giving breath of God work in a healing, cleansing way in your body-self ... in your emotional-self ... in your spirit-self ... Let the rhythm of taking in newness and healing ... and letting go of built-up tensions and stress ... take root in this time of meditation ... Know that this is a force for deep inner healing that is planted in you by the Creator ... and that this is a power you may access whenever you want or need to ... The breath keeps your body open ... allowing it to do its work ... allowing the energies to flow ...

Breathe in possibility ... Breathe in the hope that the Spirit gives ... Let go of the stress and tensions that are stored in your body-self ... and in your emotional-self ... and in your spiritual-self ... Breathe in life energy ... The creating breath of God that was there from the beginning ... Breathe out whatever would block you from being fully present to this time ... Again notice your body ... If there continue to be tense places, imagine this healing breath moving directly to those spots ... unknotting the tension ... letting go ... letting be ... letting open ... letting unlock ...

As you give yourself the gift of relaxation, the gift of embodiment ... notice the inner space created by this letting go ... Notice how much this tension that has built up in you had been blocking your inner life ... your core-self ... how much it has been keeping you from being in touch with your sacred centre ... As your prepare this space, know that there is nowhere more important to be ... that there is nothing more important to do ... than to be present ... to yourself ... to the Holy Presence ... to the Spirit ... to your deep silent centre ...

Imagine in your mind's eye ... the picture of a garden ... It is a walled garden ... very large ... containing many different kinds of trees ... and shrubs ... and flowers ... Notice the colours and the fragrance ... Notice the many paths that there are in this garden ... many different interconnecting pathways ... There are many other people in this garden ... many who work there as gardeners ... caring for the various plants and trees ... Many others that are also walking the paths ...

Imagine yourself in this garden ... walking along one of the paths ... Allow a question to come into your mind — perhaps a question about the garden, or one of the plants ... Perhaps it is not a question directly about the garden at all ... Ask your question of one of the people you meet ... and allow yourself to receive an answer ... Ask another question of another person in the garden ... and again experience yourself open to receiving the answer that is given ... How do you feel about the answer you have received? ... How do you feel about asking? ...

Now allow the Spirit to plant in you an even deeper question ... actually something more like a really deep desire ... a desire that wells up from very deep inside you ... a question that is something you need to know just for you ... Allow this desire to grow in you until it becomes like a treasure that means more than anything else in the garden ... Experience a feeling of seeking that is so strong that you know it can only come from the Holy ... And as you seek, let yourself also be filled with the knowing that you will somehow find it ... somewhere ...

As you are seeking ... notice a door in the wall of the garden ... You keep being drawn to this door ... Your eyes keep coming back to this door ... You feel a strong pull rising in you to open the door and go through to discover what is on the other side ... It is as if you know that this is connected with the desire that has been growing in you ... But you also feel the pull to stay and enjoy the beautiful garden that you already know ... Increasingly you keep wondering what is on the other side of that door? ... What do you most desire to find on the other side of that door?... on the other side of the wall?...

Knock on the door ... Is there someone who answers? ... Does the door open up for you? ... What do you ask for? ... What do you experience on the other side of the wall?...

Take the time you need to live your experience ... then gradually draw yourself back to this place ... gradually get in touch with the body ... Take some deep breaths ... Make some gentle movements with your toes and fingers ... some circles with your head ... Become aware of your body as it touches the chair ... the floor ... and open your eyes when you feel ready.

SHARING

JOURNALLING/DRAWING

DEBRIEFING
Ask those who wish to share what happened for them in the meditation:
   • What questions did you find yourself asking?
   • What answers did you receive from people in the garden?
   • What desire finally drove you to knock at the door?
   • What happened when you did?

CLOSURE

Sing: Seek Ye First the Kingdom (verses 1 and 2).

16

PREPARING FOR NEW BIRTH
THE ANNUNCIATION: AN ADVENT MEDITATION

INTRODUCTION

PREPARATION

- paper and pens/pencils/drawing materials
- painting or icon of the annunciation or Mary and the infant Christ
- photos of pregnant women or frightened young women

SCRIPTURE: LUKE 1:26–38

REFLECTION

I feel that it is a terrible waste of a powerful Advent image, when the lectionary leaves any mention of Mary's pregnancy until the very last week of Advent. By then we are usually fully launched into special Christmas services, and the story of the Annunciation gets lost in the shuffle.

Anyone who has dealt with pregnancy, first or second hand, knows the waiting involved, and the whole mix of feelings and issues: anxiety, expectancy, hopefulness, fear, uncertainty, joy, wonder, inadequacy, and many more. One's whole life is changed, and so is the life of those around who are affected. An incredible adjustment is required to the new reality that is coming, yet is already present in expectation and hope in a very tangible way in a woman's body. I like to bring in the Annunciation story early into the Advent season to lift up these dynamics.

Advent needs to celebrate spiritual pregnancy. It is important that it be done in a way that is sensitive to the fact that in your community you will have infertile couples, those who have chosen to have no children, those who have been part of a choice to end pregnancy, those whose pregnancies have ended through no choice of their own, those who have had children they were not prepared for and wish they had never had, those who are male, single, elderly, or are part of families that are not traditional.

I have found that, when there is recognition that pregnancy brings with it all kinds of experiences, memories, and conflicted feelings, people of all types seem to be able to relate to the invitation to bear new life — even men! For many, doing such a meditation has been the first time that they have ever thought of themselves as a vehicle for the sacred to come into the world; as a means for some incarnation of the Divine that is longing to find birth. It is easy as well to connect with the ambiguous feelings most of us have around such an invitation.

Remembering and connecting with personal and family birth stories and pregnancy stories can touch into some powerful healing material.

GATHERING

a) Use Ann Johnson's "Magnificat of Waiting" from *Miryam of Nazareth*.[15] Either ask participants to close their eyes while you read it to them after a period of silence, or have copies available for people to read and reflect on in silence. Where does this reading connect with you? Share around the circle.

b) Remember your own experiences of discovering you were pregnant or that someone close to you was pregnant. What feelings were there?

c) How do you think your mother and father felt when they discovered they were pregnant with you? How do you feel about this?

d) If you were to discover right now that you were pregnant (even if you are male), what feelings and reactions would be aroused?

e) If someone you knew came to you and told you she was pregnant and it was by the Holy Spirit, what would be your reaction?

f) Advent is a time for all Christians to become pregnant (male or female, young or ancient, fertile or infertile). In Advent we are invited to bear the seed of God, the Sacred Child. We are invited to bring to birth the incarnation of God's presence in the world.
   - Do you have any sense in your own life of where you are being invited, and maybe challenged, to give room for some seed of God to be born in you?
   - What are you being invited to give birth to in this Advent season?

MEDITATION

Shut your eyes and let your body relax ... let it sink into the chair or into the floor ... Let yourself be held up ... supported by the chair or floor ... You do not need to do the work of holding up your body ... you can let it be supported ... you can let go and relax ... Begin to notice your breathing ... Breath is essential to living ... We are told in scripture that it was God's breath that created all that is ... It has the power for cleansing and healing not only our physical system ... but also our emotional and spiritual lives ... Notice the breath as it begins at the tip of your nose ... Feel the cool air as it moves through your nostrils ... Follow it as it moves across the roof of your mouth ... Follow it as it goes down into your windpipe ... Follow it as it goes through your bronchial tubes into your lungs ... Notice where it goes in your lungs ... How deeply is the breath of life moving within you? ... Gradually allow your breath to move more deeply in your body ... Let it open up space inside you ... space to meet the Holy ... space for you to BE ...

Gradually allow yourself to soften and flow with the breath ... Let your shoulders fall and relax as you breathe into the part of your lungs high up in your shoulders ... Let your tummy muscles let go as you let the breath move deeply into your whole torso ... Notice what it feels like to be in your body-self as this happens...

Now move through your body tensing and letting go of the muscles. Begin with your feet ... Tense the muscles of your feet then to let go ... Experience what it feels like to let go and to relax ... Move up to the calves ... tense ... hold tight ... then relax ... let go ... Move up to the thighs ...tense ... hold tight ... then relax ... let go ... Move to the hips and pelvis ... tense ... hold tight ... then relax ... let go ... to the abdomen ... the stomach and middle back ... tense ... hold tight ... then relax ... let go ... to the upper back ... tense ... hold tight ... then relax ... let go ... to the shoulders ... the arms ... the hands ... tense ... hold tight ... then relax ... let go ... to the neck ... the head ... tense ... hold tight ... then relax ... let go...

Notice the feeling of letting go ... of relaxing ... of well-being ... Let the breath move freely and deeply into your body ... Let yourself come to your sacred centre to the still place inside ...

Imagine yourself in a sacred place ... a place where you feel safe and connected ... a place where you can go to meet the Holy ... As you look around
what do you see? ... Is it indoors or outdoors? ... Is it day or night? ... Notice
the colours in this place ... Notice any sounds ... any smells ... any textures ...
Let yourself really be in this place as you prepare yourself to meet a messenger of the Sacred ...

Become aware that the messenger, the one who carries insight and meaning
from the Holy One is arriving in this place where you are ... What do you
notice about the messenger? ... Is it a person? ... or more just a sense of
presence? ... Mary felt quite afraid when the angel came to her ... How do
you feel about this messenger's arrival? ... Try to get a sense, or an image, or
a feel for the presence of God's messenger in the meeting place ...

Mary's angel invited her to bear a child ... What seed of God does the
messenger invite you to take into the core of your being in this time of your
life? ... Listen for what God might be asking you to allow to grow in you at
this time? ... How do you react to this suggestion? ... How would it feel for
you to express what you are feeling? ... any misgivings? ... any uncertainties?
... What happens when you allow yourself to be honest about how you feel
about this invitation or request? ...

What would it feel like for you to accept this call? ... Let yourself imagine
what would happen inside you if you said yes ... what changes would
happen in you? ... What would you need in order to be able to say yes? ... Let
yourself imagine what would happen to your world if you were to say yes to
the invitation to bear God's seed? ... What would your bearing of the seed
of God in your own context be? ... What might happen? ... What might
change? ... Try to get a picture, or a sense of what this might be like ... How
would this affect your relationships? ... Picture a relationship — or more
than one relationship — that would be affected by this new birth you have
allowed ...

Let yourself imagine what would happen in the heart of God ... What
would it feel like for you to refuse? ... Continue to dialogue with the mes-

senger of the Holy in whatever way is necessary for you ... Ask for what you would need in order to say yes, if this is your choice...

When you feel ready, gradually draw yourself back to an awareness of the place where you began ... gradually begin again to notice your breathing, and your body-self ... Begin to draw yourself back to the group ... back to this place ... and when you feel ready ... open your eyes.

S H A R I N G

Journalling/Drawing

Debriefing

Ask participants to share:
- What happened for you in this meditation journey?
- How did you react to the invitation from the messenger?
- What were you being invited by God to bring to life?

C L O S U R E

Sing: To a Maid Whose Name Was Mary

17

SHARING IN SOLIDARITY:
MARY VISITS ELIZABETH
AN ADVENT MEDITATION

INTRODUCTION

PREPARATION

- paper and pens/pencils/drawing materials
- painting of Mary and Elizabeth or Mary and the infant Christ
- photos of pregnant women or frightened young women

SCRIPTURE: LUKE 1:39–56

REFLECTION

Mary's life was turned upside down by the invitation to bear the Christ. She is a young woman with plans for her life. And suddenly, something outrageous and shocking happens. She is pregnant but is not yet married. It is not necessary to take the story literally, to try to put oneself into this frightened young woman's position.

In Matthew, it is made clear that Joseph was going to do the honourable thing. He was going to cut off the engagement quietly and not demand that his honour be recompensed with her stoning or some other humiliating punishment. In Matthew, it was only through the wisdom of a dream that Joseph was able to stand by Mary. I wonder what must that have done to their relationship? He had been willing to get rid of her.

I wonder how Mary's family reacted to the news of the unexpected pregnancy? I wonder how the town gossip mill reacted? What happened to Mary's mother and sisters and brothers when they walked through the town?

Mary did what so many young women in "trouble" have done. She got out of town. She went to the home of her cousin Elizabeth, far away. When she was given the invitation to birth, she was also given what she needed for support. She was given the information that her older cousin Elizabeth was also pregnant in similar strange circumstances. Mary went to be with another woman who had much the same experience. Together they had to try to make sense out of their pregnancies.

A little-noted part of the story that has always amused me is that Zechariah, Elizabeth's husband, who was a temple priest, was struck dumb, unable to speak during the entire visit. I have the delightful image of two women, talking a mile a minute, sharing concerns and information, sharing stories and worries, trying on different ways of understanding what it might all mean. All the while, the priest, the theologian, is unable to speak a word into the situation. He must have been very frustrated indeed!

Mary goes back to her roots in the Hebrew tradition, to Hannah, another woman who had dealt with childbirth in unusual circumstances. What we call the Magnificat, Mary's Song, shows a self-understanding very much in that context. She sings of the upside-down making God who scatters the proud, who brings the mighty down from their thrones, who lifts up the lowly and fills the hungry with good things.

This new birth is not just about a cuddly baby who would give people a warm glow. Incarnation was, and is a powerful force for changing the world in very concrete ways. It changes how we think about our own embodiment, and it changes how we feel about worth and power in the life of the world.

Mary was a young woman, probably just a teen. She must have been very frightened and felt so alone as she faced the birth of this first child with, it would seem, not a lot of support. She needed to be with someone who understood how she felt. She needed to be with an older woman.

Scripture tells us that she stayed with Elizabeth for three months, most likely until John was born. She must have learned a lot about pregnancy and birthing and nursing during this time. She also seems to have learned to see meaning in her unsettling experience, and to have found ways to talk about it that gave her the strength to carry on. She was given support to strengthen her at a time of crisis, with the result that, after three months, she was able to return home and deal with what met her there.

GATHERING

a) Tell the story of the visit to Elizabeth in the manner of the reflection. Ask for reactions. What does this evoke in you?

b)   Sometimes only someone who has walked the same walk is able to help.
   •   Have you had experiences in your life, where you have needed someone
       who had "been there" for support?
   •   Perhaps you were the one someone else needed for support because of
       your experience. What was that like?

c)   How have crises, or stressful experiences that you have lived through, helped
    you to be more understanding or compassionate to others?

d)   Mary reached back into the stories of her Hebrew tradition to try to make
    sense of the chaos that was happening in her life. Are there parts of the
    Hebrew/Christian tradition that have been helpful to you in times of crisis as
    you have tried to find words for understanding the meaning of what was
    happening in your own life?

MEDITATION

Shut your eyes and let your body relax ... let it sink into the chair or into the
floor ... Let yourself be held up ... supported by the chair or floor ... You do
not need to do the work of holding up your body ... you can let it be supported ... you can let go and relax ... Begin to notice your breathing ...
Breath is essential to living ... We are told in scripture that it was God's
breath that created all that is ... It has the power for cleansing and healing
not only our physical system ... .but also our emotional and spiritual lives ...
Notice the breath as it begins at the tip of your nose ... the cool air as it
moves through your nostrils ... Follow it as it moves across the roof of your
mouth ... Follow it as it goes down into your windpipe ... Follow it as it goes
through your bronchial tubes into your lungs ... Notice where it goes in
your lungs ... How deeply is the breath of life moving within you? ... Gradually allow your breath to move more deeply in your body ... Let it open up
space inside you ... space to meet the Holy ... space for you to BE ...

Gradually allow yourself to soften and flow with the breath ... Let your
shoulders fall and relax as you breathe into the part of your lungs high up
in your shoulders ... Let your tummy muscles let go as you let the breath
move deeply into your whole torso ... Notice what it feels like to be in your
body-self as this happens...

Now move through your body tensing and letting go of the muscles. Begin with your feet ... Tense the muscles of your feet then to let go ... Experience what it feels like to let go and to relax ... Move up to the calves ... tense ... hold tight ... then relax ... let go ... Move up to the thighs ... tense ... hold tight ... then relax ... let go ... Move to the hips and pelvis ... tense ... hold tight ... then relax ... let go ... to the abdomen ... the stomach and middle back ... tense ... hold tight ... then relax ... let go ... to the upper back ... tense ... hold tight ... then relax ... let go ... to the shoulders ... the arms ... the hands ... tense ... hold tight ... then relax ... let go ... to the neck ... the head ... tense ... hold tight ... then relax ... let go...

Notice the feeling of letting go ...of relaxing ... of well-being ... Let the breath move freely and deeply into your body ... Let yourself come to your sacred centre to the still place inside ... to the inner space for meeting the Sacred...

Imagine yourself in a time of crisis ... a time both of danger but of opportunity ... of possibility ... It may be a time that you have actually experienced, that you re-enter for this meditation ... or it may be a crisis that you imagine ... or one that you are facing right now ... Get in touch with the anxiety and the fear associated with the difficult time ... Get in touch with the possibility, with the expectancy in the situation as well ...

Be in touch with the need to have someone with whom you can really share this experience ... Someone who can understand what you are going through ... Someone who can really be there for you ... Someone who can witness your struggle, and offer caring and advice (if that is appropriate) while you try to work it through ...

As you are in touch with this longing for another to be with you, try to get an image in your mind of which person that might be ... It may be someone you know ... or it may be someone you call up in your imagination ... What kind of person would be helpful for you in your time of need? ... What are the qualities that would make you choose that person?...

Imagine yourself going on a journey to meet with that person ... imagine the way you are travelling ... Imagine how long it will take you ... Be in touch with the feelings that rise up in you as you prepare to meet this person ... Imagine yourself arriving where you will meet that person ... Notice how you are greeted ... Are you welcomed? ... Are they surprised to see you? ... Do you feel the warmth you had hoped would be there? ...

Imagine the person sitting you down in a comfortable chair ... making you a cup of tea ... bringing a flowering plant near to you ... lighting a candle ... asking you to share a moment of silence with them ... then inviting you to talk about what you need to talk about ... Are you able to pour out the pain and the fear that is in you? ... How does the other receive this? ... What do they do? ... What do they say? ...

How does it feel to be able to share your crisis in a safe place? ... in a place where you experience acceptance? ... in a place where you are understood? ... in a place where you know that the other wants only what is best for you? ... How does it feel to be received in this way? ... Do you find it easy to trust the other with the really deep things, or do you approach the subject cautiously? ...

Is there any wisdom that the other person has for you? ... Is there any insight that can help you as you work things through? ... Allow the other to offer you the love and support you need in this time ... Allow yourself to experience the healing power of sacred friendship ... of communion with another who loves and cares for you ... What happens to your soul? ... your mind? ... your body? ... as you receive this sacred friendship ... As you pre-pare to leave this place, how does this affect how you will face the crisis when you return? ... Is there any difference in how you feel about yourself? ... about the crisis you have to face? ...

Thank the person who has been supportive to you in any way that feels appropriate to you both ... Take a deep breath ... gradually draw yourself back into an awareness of your body as it is sitting on the chair (or lying down) ... As you feel ready, begin to draw yourself gently back to this room

... Make some movements with your toes and fingers ... perhaps some gentle head rolls, as you come back to this place to meet those who have taken this journey alongside you ... Open your eyes when you feel ready to do so.

SHARING

JOURNALLING/DRAWING

DEBRIEFING

Ask participants to share what happened for them in the meditation:

- What kind of person was your sacred friend in this meditation experience?
- What did you need help with?
- What kind of support did you receive?
- How does this affect how you will face the problem you were dealing with in the meditation?

CLOSURE

Sing: She Walked in the Summer

18

FACING INTO FEAR
AND HEALING

INTRODUCTION
PREPARATION
- paper and pens/pencils/drawing materials
- candle
- cross
- picture of the Aesculapian medical symbol of a snake on a rod or picture of a snake
- bowl of water

SCRIPTURE: PSALM 137, NUMBERS 21:4–9, JOHN 3:14–21

REFLECTION

The lament of the exiles in Babylon raises many fears; fear of never again being able to go home; fear that they will never feel at home in this foreign land; fear that God has abandoned and forgotten them; fear of what the powerful captors will demand; fear that they will forget Jerusalem, forget the temple, forget where they belong; fear that they will never be able to feel joy or to sing God's song again with any meaning; fear that the weeping will never end.

In Numbers, the people of Israel are sick and tired of wandering around in the wilderness after they have left slavery in Egypt. They are afraid of the wilderness; afraid of dying in this alien place; afraid of not having enough food; afraid of not having enough water; afraid their leader Moses does not have a clue where he is going; afraid of the anger and frustration that they have expressed to Moses and to God; afraid of poisonous snakes whose bites are killing them.

In the story, Moses is told by God to take a snake, the very thing that is causing them so much grief and pain, and to place it on a pole where it becomes a source of healing!

Although we are all familiar with the snake associated with evil in tradition, Carl Jung notes that the symbol of the snake, in almost all cultures, is linked with transcendence, with eternal life and immortality. Snakes renew themselves by shedding their skins. They must shed them, in fact, in order to grow.

An interesting sidelight on this whole story is the close association between serpents and the goddess religion that prevailed in the Near East at that time. Various Indo-European invaders from Egypt to Assyria, including the Hebrews themselves, brought war-like faiths to the region. These were at odds with the long-standing, and continuing norm, of the worship of a supreme female deity — the peaceful, fertile earth goddess. One of the key symbols of this deity was the serpent, representing knowledge of the powerful medicines to be found throughout nature, in both plants and animals, like snake venom (which is the source of its own anti-venom).

The snake was also the symbol of healing in the Greek temples of Aesculapius. When one was sick, one would go to the temple and spend the night. The snake would come and whisper in one's ear what to do for healing. The ancient story from Numbers and this Greek tradition converge with the symbol of a snake on a rod, which is the symbol of the modern medical profession.

In *Mystical Christianity*, Episcopal priest and Jungian therapist John Sanford has a section on the snake, in which he points out that there was a Gnostic Christian sect that worshipped the snake in the Genesis 3 creation story, seeing it as the Christ symbol in the story.[16] The snake, like Christ, was the one who brought consciousness and was cursed for doing it. How close this is to the ancient story of Prometheus as well.

The Gospel of John compares facing the execution of Jesus with Moses lifting the bronze serpent in the wilderness. Moses took the very thing that was biting the people, put it on a pole, and placed it firmly before their eyes. He said, "Look at it — See the healing power of God coming to you out of the snake." Jesus on the cross has become a symbol that forces us to look death and evil in the face — but also to discover the life that even this horror cannot destroy. It points us into the depths of horror where human beings torture one another — into that abyss of anguish where we experience what it is to be abandoned and where we come to know that human life doesn't make sense. But it points us deeper still, so that we see in spite of the horror and anguish the new life that comes.

As we dare to face into fear — dare to be present to fear, anger, estrangement — we open ourselves to the challenge of transformation, to healing and new life. Healing comes when we face what is crippling us.

GATHERING

a)   Ask participants to think about a time in their lives when they overcame a fear. What happened?

b)   Suggest that participants might wish to take a few minutes to journal about their fear, then to share with one other person as they feel comfortable. Some may wish to draw their fear, to get a sense of the colour and form of it.

c)   Share parts of the reflection that you feel would help to set the context for the meditation. I would tend to talk about the scriptures, rather than to read them in detail, if this were a group at a time other than the morning service. The passage from Numbers is a good story. The imagery from the river in Babylon is merely a background setting for the meditation. If you do not choose to use this scripture, leave out the references to the river of Babylon at the beginning of the meditation (in parentheses).

d)   Remind those who are doing this meditation, that they are always free to enter only as deeply as is appropriate for them, and to deal with only the fear that is possible for them to deal with at this time and in this context. Participants are always in charge of how far they wish to go in meditation.

MEDITATION

Shut your eyes ... let yourself begin to connect with this body-self that you are ... this holy temple ... Many of us spend our whole lives disconnected from our body-self ... We take our body for granted ... We do not recognize it as created in God's image ... as a source of wisdom and profound knowing ... Ask your body to teach you its wisdom as your relax ... as you tell your mind that it doesn't need to help you for the next while ... that it is good for you to relax and just be for the next little while ... Tell your mind that it can take a rest ... that you appreciate that it is trying to help, but that just for now you want to be fully present to your body-self ... and to its wisdom ... As you begin to pay attention to your body, do you notice places where tension is stored up? ... where your muscles are in tight knots? ... As you scan your body, from the top of your head to the bottom of your feet ... notice if there are tender places ... sore spots ... and send compassion to these places in your body, thanking them for the hard work they are doing

... perhaps offering to pay more attention to what they are telling you in the future ... Befriend the places of pain in your body...

Become aware of your breathing ... of the life-sustaining breath that goes on all of the time ... even when we are unaware ... Notice if you are breathing with only a small part of your lungs, or whether you are taking the breath deeply into your whole being ... down to the bottom of your lungs ... Breathe with your whole torso ... your whole body... Take the breath of life up to the tops of your shoulders ... a place where many of us store stress and the heavy loads we are carrying ... Notice if your tummy moves in and out as you inhale and exhale ... the way a baby's does when it is breathing naturally...

Notice where you are tightened up ... not fully open to the breath of life... Let your body relax ... let the tension flow out of your body through your feet ... Begin to allow your breath to move deeper into your being ... taking the breath deep down into your belly ... creating inner space ... Breathe in deeply the healing presence of the Spirit ... the goodness and grace of God ... Take it right into your centre ... With each breath out, allow the breath to carry away the toxins that have built up ... the physical poisons that need to be cleansed ... Let it also carry out the emotional poisons that have been stored in your body ... the pains and angers that need to be let go ... Let the healing breath gently caress the wounded places ... let the life-giving breath of God work in a healing, cleansing way in your body-self ... in your emotional-self ... in your spirit-self ... Let the rhythm of taking in newness and healing ... and letting go of built-up tensions and stress ... take root in this time of meditation ... Know that this is a force for deep inner healing that is planted in you by the Creator ... and that this is a power you may access whenever you want, or need to ... The breath keeps your body open ... allowing it to do its work ... allowing the energies to flow ...

Breathe in possibility ... Breathe in the hope that the Spirit gives ... Let go of the stress and tensions that are stored in your body-self ... and in your emotional-self ... and in your spiritual-self ... Breathe in life energy ... The creating breath of God that was there from the beginning ... Breathe out whatever would block you from being fully present to this time ... Again notice your body ... If there continue to be tense places, imagine this healing breath moving directly to those spots ... unknotting the tension ... letting go ... letting be ... letting open ... letting unlock...

As you give yourself the gift of relaxation, the gift of embodiment ... notice the inner space created by this letting go ... Notice how much this tension that has built up in you had been blocking your inner life ... your core-self ... how much it has been keeping you from being in touch with your sacred centre ... As your prepare this space, know that there is nowhere more important to be ... that there is nothing more important to do ... than to be present ... to yourself ... to the Holy Presence ... to the Spirit ... to your deep silent centre...

Imagine yourself beside a river ... (beside your river of Babylon) ... the river that you go to when you are looking for a place to get grounded ... a safe place to feel your pain ... to feel your fear ... a sacred place that grounds you with a sense of timelessness ... of life flowing on ... of the flow of life being larger and more eternal than your own feelings ... Look around you and notice the colours ... the textures ... the smells ... the sounds ... Is the sun shining or is it night? ... Are you alone? ... or do you wish to have trusted others with you? ... those who care deeply for you ... who know you and love and support you exactly as you are ...

As you ground yourself in this place allow the Spirit to call to your mind or imagination a particular fear that you have ... You may not choose the hardest one. ... It may be more appropriate for you to pay attention to a lesser one ... Ask God to help bring to mind the fear that God feels you are ready to deal with now ... It may be about something that is happening in your life right now ... or it may be an underlying fear that you know to be a part of your story ...

Try to think of a particular time when you felt that fear ... Call to mind the circumstances that were going on in your life ... Think about the situation that triggered it ...

As you have in mind this situation, can you remember a time in your past when you felt like this? ... Are there any connections? ... What effect does this fear have on you? ... Does it paralyze you? ... close you off? ... make you want to run away? ... make you invisible? ... make you feel like a helpless child? ... Make you angry and aggressive? ... make you want to reach out to be held and supported? ... Perhaps there is some other reaction you have to this fear ... Allow yourself know what happens inside you when you experience this fear ...

Notice how much energy it takes to deal with it ... Do you have any space in your life to love or to play when you are in the grips of this fear? ... Do you have any flexibility or ability to see possibility? ... Where do you store this fear in your body? ...

Now imagine the light of Christ as healing, loving energy, flowing into this fear you have been facing into ... Let the light of Christ's all-seeing, all-loving truth penetrate this place of fear to show it for what it really is ... What does this fear have to teach you about yourself as you are able to look at it in the healing light of the Spirit ... Let this healing light help you understand and experience what the real source of this fear is ... where you learned to be afraid in this way ... where you learned to respond with fear ... Respect this fear ... honour the person who learned this response of fear ... Let the light bathe the fear with healing ... Let the light bathe the memory with healing ... bathe the hurt with healing ... bathe the frightened child within ...

Let the light melt the places in your body where this fear, this tension has been frozen ... locked up ... As the fear releases and you let go, feel the energy transformed into love ... Feel the energy for life ... for loving ... flow freely in your body and in your spirit, as the Spirit begins to heal the fear that has kept you in bondage ... Let the healing light work in whatever way is right for you today ... Let it offer whatever understanding is appropriate for you to have now about this fear ... You may experience the healing without ever understanding what it is about ... Let the healing light surround you with confidence that you are deeply loved to the core of your being by the Source of Life who knows you in a deep and intimate way ...

Notice again the river of life beside which you have been sitting ... it still flows on ... It continues its journey to the sea ... a journey that has been going on before you lived and will continue after you are dead ... Take comfort in this reminder of the ongoing flow of life that is so much bigger than your own emotional flow ... You may wish to dip your hand into that water and let it pour over you as you give thanks for healing ...

Gradually allow yourself to get back in touch with your body-self ... Get in touch with your breathing again and take some deep breaths, paying particular attention to the breath out ... as you allow it to release whatever needs to be let go ... Make some gentle movements with your toes and fingers ... some gentle circles with your head, and gradually draw yourself back to this place ... Open your eyes as you feel ready.

SHARING
JOURNALLING/DRAWING

DEBRIEFING
Some questions that might help begin the discussion would be:
- What was the Holy like for you in this meditation?
- Were you able to get any insight or healing for a fear you have been dealing with?
- Is there any next step that you feel called to take at this time?

CLOSURE

After debriefing and sharing, there are several options for closure that could be significant. Choose one, based on how participants are feeling.

a) A ritual using the water in the worship centre — dip your fingers into it and anoint your forehead (or heart or other parts of their body). Words might be used while doing this such as "I honour my healing journey." You may suggest these or other words, or each person may wish to use their own affirmation that is meaningful to their experience.

b) Make a circle holding hands. Sing Amazing Grace, Spirit of the Living God, or Peace is Flowing Like a River (using the words "God's healing's flowing like a river" for one of the verses).

c) Have circle prayer where participants offer their own prayers, if this comfort-
    able in your setting, or share the Lord's Prayer together. Offer a blessing to
    one another and share the peace of Christ (always remembering to remind
    those present that there are those who feel comfort from hugs and touches,
    and those for whom this is difficult).

Do check with participants as they leave. It will be particularly important to notice
anyone who did not speak out in the debriefing time. Make yourself available for
anyone who would need to talk after this meditation. It may unlock issues for
people that they might need help dealing with. Some will feel comfortable doing
this in the group. Others may prefer to do it one-on-one.

19

CROSSING TO THE OTHER SIDE
LETTING GO AND MOVING ON

INTRODUCTION

PREPARATION
- paper and pens/pencils/drawing materials
- candle
- photos of boats at sea, harbours, boats loading at dock
- symbols that suggest journey, e.g. map, small suitcase

SCRIPTURE
Choose one of the scriptures below, or use another scripture that uses the theme of letting go, risking journey:
- Matthew 6:19–34 (from the sermon on the mount)
- Matthew 13:47–48 (the parable of the dragnet)
- Matthew 20:16–23 (the rich young ruler)
- Matthew 4:18–22 or Luke 5:1–11 (the call of the disciples)
- Luke 9:23–25 (the conditions of discipleship)

With references to any of the many scriptures in which Jesus gets in a boat and crosses to the other side, e.g. Matthew 9:1 ff., Matthew 8:18–23, Matthew 14:13, 22–35.

REFLECTION
This meditation would be an appropriate deepening of many scriptures for it works with Jesus' core message of the journey of conversion from conventional life to transformed "reign-of-God" living. The passage suggested from the sermon on the mount may not immediately suggest journey, however, it contrasts two differ-

ent states of being and being controlled ("mastered") by opposing sets of values. To move from being "mastered" by fear, wealth, status, economic security, and other treasures valued on this earth, to being grounded and rooted in reign of God values and spirituality requires letting go, embracing transformation, and risking moving on.

I have always been struck in reading the passage about anxiety in the face of needs, with the comment that God already knows that we really do need basic things. It is simply that these needs are not to become the focal point of our lives or the organizing principle around which everything else we do is centred. Apparently Jesus is trying to get us to change our focus and our obsession with these needs. By grounding ourselves to the core, in the reign of God, our other needs fall into an appropriate level of priority. It's about letting go and moving on.

The same theme is very present in the parable of the dragnet, where it is necessary to choose what to keep and what to let go. The parable of the wealthy ruler also points to the tension and the struggle of letting go and moving on. He is on the threshold of transformation, but cannot make the next step at the time Jesus encounters him. The stories of the call of the disciples are not very developed in terms of the psychological struggle of leaving and following, however, these stories certainly evoke that tension for most of us when we imagine ourselves being called to leave everything behind and follow a whole new path.

Much of Jesus' teaching is about making journeys — the journey that our souls make as we grow from one state of being to another. Many of Jesus' teachings are about the need to let go of the way things are, in order to journey towards what God calls us to be. Jesus calls us to a conversion of our core-selves and values, to selves and values rooted in the Reign of God. This calls us to journey from the structures of life and forms of security that we have built up around ourselves to move towards a vision where a different kind of experience is possible, a different set of values exists. This journey requires great courage. As Jesus discovered, some were at a point of readiness to embrace it; others could embrace the first steps of the journey; some were already a long way along; others were so locked up in security and fear that they could not risk being open to such possibilities at the time he encountered them.

As we engage in this process, we need to see the truth about ourselves, but I do not believe it is helpful, or empowering, to look through judgemental, self-destructive lenses. In the meditation, I suggest that we look through the knowing and loving eyes of Christ. It is a journey to allow the truth that is in us to grow and to be seen in the light of Christ's presence. We are only able to make a radical, core transformation when we are grounded in the love and grace and invitation of God.

We cannot take all the steps on the journey at one time. We can only go as far as we are able before resting and gathering strength for the next leg of the journey. Jesus seemed to have been very aware of this in his teachings. He always met people where they were and invited them to grow and move onward as they were able. This meditation asks us to look at where we are in that process. There is no shame in needing to abandon the journey if we need more time and experience in the place where we now are before we are able to continue the journey.

The questions about what we are ready to let go of can only be asked once we are already on the journey, at sea, separated from the familiar shore, yet still some distance from the unknown shore to which we are headed. In a small boat, in the middle of the sea, Christ asks us about what baggage we are carrying. Is it out of habit? Can it be let go? Have we grown beyond it enough to release it?

GATHERING

a)   Reflect on preparing for a journey you have taken:
   - How did you prepare?
   - What kinds of things did you remember to take with you?
   - How did you discern what to leave behind?

b)   Think about what it is like to journey with excess baggage:
   - What happens when you do this?
   - How does it affect your journey?
   - Think about some excess baggage that you have been carrying in your own life that has outlived its usefulness:
     - What baggage is weighing your journey down?
     - What would you like to let go?
     - What would it take to help you let go?

c)   Introduce the theme of journey and letting go. Read the scripture chosen slowly, perhaps having different voices read it more than once, emphasizing different things each time. Set the scripture in context using some of the material from the reflection.

d)   Let participants know that this meditation is one that they can do for themselves many times. The meditation deals with a process of growing — and this journey is not something we accomplish and complete fully in one single meditation.

MEDITATION

Shut your eyes and let your body relax ... Let it sink into the chair or into the floor ... Let yourself be held up ... supported by the chair or floor ... You do not need to do the work of holding up your body ... You can let it be supported ... You can let go and relax...

Begin to notice your breathing ... Breath is essential to living ... It was God's breath, we are told, that created all that is ... It has the power for cleansing and healing not only our physical system ... but also our emotional and spiritual lives ... Notice the breath as it begins at the tip of your nose ... Feel the cool air as it moves through your nostrils ... Follow it as it moves across the roof of your mouth ... Follow it as it goes down into your windpipe ... Follow it as it goes through your bronchial tubes into your lungs ... Notice where it goes into your lungs ... How deeply is the breath of life moving within you? ...

Gradually allow your breath to move more deeply into your being ... Let it open up space inside you ... space to meet the Holy ... space for you to BE ...

Gradually allow yourself to soften and flow with the breath ... Let your shoulders fall and relax as you breathe into the part of your lungs high up in your shoulders ... Let your tummy muscles relax and let go as you let the breath move deeply into your whole torso ... Notice what it feels like to be in your body-self as this happens ... Notice the feeling of letting go ... of relaxing ... of well-being ... of inner space for meeting the Holy ...

Pick one place (either the tip of the nose or a place in the lungs) in which to simply observe the breath as it passes ... in and out ... in and out ... Let yourself come to your sacred centre ... to the still place inside ...

Imagine that you are going on a journey ... It is a spiritual journey ... It is a journey that you really desire to go on ... Allow that desire to rise up in you ... Allow the desire for journey ... the desire to be closer and more deeply connected to God grow in you, until it almost wells up from inside you ...

You arrive at a boat dock with a bag that contains what you feel you cannot leave behind ... Be aware of what is in your bag ...

Smell the sea air ... Notice the small boat that will carry you on your journey ... Are there others around? ... Now become aware of the presence of Christ who is there ... Christ is the One who has invited you on this journey ... Experience the delight and hope that is in Christ as you arrive to begin this journey ... Christ invites you into the boat ... and tells you that it is time to leave ... You discover that Christ will be with you on this whole journey ... Notice how you feel about that invitation ... about that Presence journeying with you ...

Now the boat has moved away from the shore, but you are still able to see the shore you have left very clearly ... You are on the sea ... The boat feels overloaded, but up to this time Christ has been controlling the boat ...

Now the water is deeper and the sea more open ... Christ says that we cannot continue with such a load. Even if the boat might manage it, this is a spiritual journey ... and the bag contains parts of yourself that belong on the shore that we have left behind ... These parts of yourself, have nothing to do with the place where we are going ... You will need a whole different way of being there ...

Christ tells you to open your bag and look inside at what is there ... Then you will have the choice of what you want, or are able to do ... It will be your choice and decision about whether this is the time to continue the journey, or to return to the shore you left ... for some further growth there ...

Now that you are on the journey, already some distance from the shore you have left ... open your bag and look carefully at its contents ... Christ tells you to allow spiritual light to shine through your eyes as you look at this parcel ... Allow the light of unconditional love to look at the truth about the bag and about yourself ... Christ looks deeply into your soul with great love and compassion, but also with invitation ... Look deeply into these eyes that contain no judgement ... no rejection ... only the light of loving truth ...

Christ speaks again and tells you to decide what you want ... Do you want to hold onto everything that is in this bag? ... You can do that and you can be taken back to shore ... This may not be the time for you to make this journey ... There will be other invitations ... other opportunities ... Or do you find that you have outgrown some of its contents? ... that some of it can be let go? ... so that you can continue on this journey ... What attitudes are in your bag that used to be useful but that are no longer helping you grow? ... Can you trust enough to let go of these things in order to continue on the journey now? ... Can you trust your own desire for this journey? ... Are you ready to go on this journey? ... You cannot take the whole of your old mind with you on this journey, because the other shore is a place where you will have to be able to think and act from a new mind ...

Are you ready to let go of what you have outgrown? ... Are you ready to let go of what has given you security in the past, but is no longer relevant since you have grown spiritually? ... Have you sufficiently outgrown these patterns of thinking to journey with Christ ... or do you need more time, more experience where you are now before you can commit yourself to the journey ... Take some time to go through what is in your bag ... and to decide...

Throw off what it is possible to let go of at this time ... Take some time with the gentle and caring Christ presence ... Let yourself receive what you need at this time ... and make the decision to either carry on the journey ... or to go back to the shore for some time ... until you are ready to begin the journey again ... Know that Christ is with you, whichever choice you make ... Once you feel ready, move on ...

Notice how you feel about what has happened for you in this meditation ... What truth does this experience with Christ offer you for your journey? ...

Let yourself gradually and gently be drawn back to this place ... Become aware of your breath ... of your body-self ... Begin to make some gentle movements with your toes and fingers ... some rolls of your head and shoulders as you draw yourself back to this place and open your eyes.

[165]

S H A R I N G

JOURNALLING/DRAWING

DEBRIEFING
Ask participants to share what happened for them in the meditation:
- What did you discover about yourself in this journey?
- What did you discover about Christ?
- What are you able to, or being invited to let go of in order to continue your spiritual journey with Christ?

C L O S U R E
Sing: I Feel the Winds of God Today or Seek Ye First the Kingdom.

20

SPIRITUAL PROTECTION
FOR THE STRUGGLE

INTRODUCTION

PREPARATION
- paper and pens/pencils/drawing materials
- copies for everyone of the Prayer of Protection used in the Closure
- candle
- open Bible
- pictures and symbols of struggle (photos of flowers in the snow or growing through pavement, a colourful cross, painting on wood, or an *arpillera* [a story tapestry made from scraps of brightly coloured cloth] from El Salvador evoking beauty and life in the face of oppression and suffering)

SCRIPTURE: EPHESIANS 6:11–20

REFLECTION

Because the Christian church has rejected its militaristic history, this particular scripture that speaks of putting on the armour of God has become politically incorrect. I am in sympathy with those who challenge the history of Christianity, which has been linked with imperialism and with the blessing of military endeavours. However, those of us who have taken on any personal demons or have taken on powers and principalities in the culture know that the struggle is very real, and we need to prepare ourselves and strengthen ourselves for that struggle.

I remember sitting in a Black church in Berkeley, California, on the 4th of July one year, listening to a very articulate preacher talk about the battle for freedom and integrity that still needed to be fought for justice for Blacks. He

[*167*]

catalogued the issues of unemployment, imprisonment of young Black males, family violence, addiction, inadequate housing, inadequate training, each time ending the litany with: "We have a battle to fight! Our freedom day has not yet come!"

There is much in our society that is unjust and requires spiritually strengthened people who can hang in for long haul struggles, often without seeing desired results. This meditation can help renew spiritual strength for the struggle of social-justice work. It can also be strengthening for our personal struggles.

Many of us have personal challenges that we have to take on as part of our healing and growth. These often require incredible courage, strength, and protection. All of us can probably identify at least one time in our lives when we have had to go up against frightening odds.

In my congregation I have many women recovering from abuse. When they have to confront an abuser, or go to court, or tell their families what has happened to them, I encourage them to surround themselves with protection. I sometimes will lead them through this meditation or one of the three following meditations.

GATHERING

a) Explain that the theme of this meditation is preparing for the struggle with spiritual protection. Talk about the worship centre as it relates to that, if you have been able to find photos or symbols of resistance and struggle.

b) Ask participants to think about a time when they felt up against frightening odds:
    - What did it feel like?
    - What did you need?
    - How did you cope?
    - What helped?

c) Read the scripture, inviting participants to look beyond the military imagery to the power of what is being said.

MEDITATION

Shut your eyes and let your body relax ... Let it sink into the chair or into the floor ... Let yourself be held up ... supported by the chair or floor ... You do not need to do the work of holding up your body ... You can let it be supported ... You can let go and relax...

Begin to notice your breathing ... Breath is essential to living ... It was God's breath, we are told, that created all that is ... It has the power for cleansing and healing not only our physical system ... but also our emotional and spiritual lives ... Notice the breath as it begins at the tip of your nose ... Feel the cool air as it moves through your nostrils ... Follow it as it moves across the roof of your mouth ... Follow it as it goes down into your windpipe ... Follow it as it goes through your bronchial tubes into your lungs ... Notice where it goes into your lungs ... How deeply is the breath of life moving within you?...

Gradually allow your breath to move more deeply into your being ... Let it open up space inside you ... space to meet the Holy ... space for you to BE ...

Gradually allow yourself to soften and flow with the breath ... Let your shoulders fall and relax as you breathe into the part of your lungs high up in your shoulders ... Let your tummy muscles relax and let go as you let the breath move deeply into your whole torso ... Notice what it feels like to be in your body-self as this happens ... Notice the feeling of letting go ... of relaxing ... of well-being ... of inner space for meeting the Holy ...

Pick one place (either the tip of the nose or a place in the lungs) in which to simply observe the breath as it passes ... in and out ... in and out ... Let yourself come to your sacred centre ... to the still place inside ...

Imagine yourself in a safe and sacred place ... a place where you will be prepared by the Spirit for your struggle ahead ... Notice the sights ... the sounds ... the smells ... the colours ... the shapes ... around you ... Notice if there are other people there with you ... Is it day or is it night?...

Allow yourself to feel the power and life-giving love and energy that are in that place ... Know that the Spirit is present here and allow that Spirit to be present to you in whatever way that happens ... What is that Spirit like for you? ... Tell this Holy Presence what you need help and support for ... Tell the Spirit what it is that you have to do, but feel fear and anxiety about ...

Now in your mind's eye ... in your imagination ... allow yourself to feel or to get a sense of the Holy's desire to give you what you need ... the strength ... the power ... the protection that you need so that you can take on the task ... Imagine yourself drawing on the strength and the power of God ... Imagine God's desire to surround your vulnerability and fearful-self with protection ... so that you will be able to stand up to opposition ... to stand up to rejection ... to stand up to attack ... to stand up to anything you might meet ... Know that the protection you need is not just physical, or intellectual ... It is also spiritual ...

Imagine God's desire for you to hold your ground ... Imagine the Spirit breathing the strength of that desire into every fibre of your being ... into the cells of your body ... into the thought patterns of your mind ... into your emotions ... into your soul ... Imagine this supporting, life-giving God placing truth around you ... till it surrounds you completely ... the belt of truth ... Imagine God's truth surrounding you ... protecting you ...

Imagine your heart and torso being protected and surrounded by God's justice ... Imagine God's justice surrounding you ... protecting your heart ... protecting your vitality ... protecting your integrity ...

Imagine God's desire for peace being placed on your feet ... strong peace ... courageous peace ... peace with justice ... shalom peace ... Imagine God's peace surrounding you ...

Imagine the Spirit offering you profound faith as protection ... faith in God ... faith in yourself as God's beloved ... faith in what you are about to do ... Imagine God's faith surrounding you ...

Next imagine the Spirit surrounding your mind with the protection of salvation ... of healing ... of making whole ... Allow it to penetrate your patterns of thinking ... your patterns of remembering ... Allow it to strengthen your mind ... Imagine God's healing salvation surrounding you ...

Imagine being given powerful words by the Spirit ... so powerful that they are like a spiritual sword that can cut through your opposition ... Imagine these powerful words from the Holy protecting you ...

Imagine yourself going to do what you have to do ... surrounded and protected by the Spirit's gifts of truth ... justice ... peace ... faith ... healing salvation ... and the spiritual power of the word ... Allow the strength and protection to flow into you ... Imagine yourself unable to fail ... Imagine yourself succeeding ...

Let yourself gradually and gently draw yourself back to this place ... Become aware of your breath ... of your body-self ... Begin to make some gentle movements with your toes and fingers ... some rolls of your head and shoulders as you draw yourself back to this place and open your eyes.

SHARING

JOURNALLING/DRAWING

DEBRIEFING

Ask participants to share what it felt like for them to experience this meditation. Suggest that they can do this meditation themselves when they need extra strength. Share the Prayer of Protection with the group, and offer copies of it to any who would wish it.

> **Prayer of Protection**
> I am created by divine love,
> I am sustained by divine love,
> I am surrounded by divine love,
> I am growing into divine love.[17]

CLOSURE

The Body Blessing (see Chapter 5).

21

CLAIMING SPIRITUAL GIFTS
WISDOM – HOPE – RESURRECTION POWER

INTRODUCTION

PREPARATION
- paper and pens/pencils/drawing materials
- candle
- a cross that is like a tree of life is a useful image of resurrection
- copies of the scripture to give out at the end
- Eugene Peterson's *The Message*[18] contains a particularly good paraphrase of the scripture

SCRIPTURE: EPHESIANS 1:17–21

REFLECTION

Many of us do not claim the gifts of the Spirit that are promised us in scripture. Some of us are afraid to claim our own power, let alone to allow ourselves to be filled with God's power. This meditation uses images from the letter to the Ephesian church to help us access inner wisdom, inner seeing of the hope for which we were created and inner re-life-ing resurrection power.

MEDITATION

Shut your eyes ... let yourself begin to connect with this body-self that you are ... this holy temple ... Many of us spend our whole lives disconnected from our body-self ... We take our body for granted ... We do not recognize it as created in God's image ... as a source of wisdom and profound knowing ... Ask your body to teach you its wisdom as your relax ... as you tell your mind that it doesn't need to help you for the next while ... that it is good for you to relax and just be for the next little while ... Tell your mind that it can take a rest ... that you appreciate that it is trying to help, but that just for now you want to be fully present to your body-self ... and to its wisdom ...

As you begin to pay attention to your body, do you notice places where tension is stored up? ... where your muscles are in tight knots? ... As you scan your body, from the top of your head to the bottom of your feet ... notice if there are tender places... sore spots ... and send compassion to these places in your body, thanking them for the hard work they are doing... perhaps offering to pay more attention to what they are telling you in the future... Befriend the places of pain in your body ...

Become aware of your breathing ... of the life-sustaining breath that goes on all of the time ... even when we are unaware ... Notice if you are breathing with only a small part of your lungs, or whether you are taking the breath deeply into your whole being ... down to the bottom of your lungs ... Breathe with your whole torso ... your whole body... Take the breath of life up to the tops of your shoulders ... a place where many of us store stress and the heavy loads we are carrying ... Notice if your tummy moves in and out as you inhale and exhale ... the way a baby's does when it is breathing naturally ...

Notice where you are tightened up ... not fully open to the breath of life ... Let your body relax ... let the tension flow out of your body through your feet ... Begin to allow your breath to move deeper into your being ... taking the breath deep down into your belly ... creating inner space ... Breathe in deeply the healing presence of the Spirit ... the goodness and grace of God ... Take it right into your centre ... With each breath out, allow the breath to carry away the toxins that have built up ... the physical poisons that need to be cleansed ... Let it also carry out the emotional poisons that have been stored in your body ... the pains and angers that need to be let go ... Let the healing breath gently caress the wounded places ... let the life-giving breath of God work in a healing, cleansing way in your body-self ... in your emotional-self ... in your spirit-self ... Let the rhythm of taking in newness and healing ... and letting go of built-up tensions and stress ... take root in this time of meditation ... Know that this is a force for deep inner healing that is planted in you by the Creator ... and that this is a power you may access whenever you want, or need to ... The breath keeps your body open ... allowing it to do its work ... allowing the energies to flow ...

Breathe in possibility ... Breathe in the hope that the Spirit gives ... Let go of the stress and tensions that are stored in your body-self ... and in your emotional-self ... and in your spiritual-self ... Breathe in life energy ... The creating breath of God that was there from the beginning ... Breathe out whatever would block you from being fully present to this time ... Again notice your body ... If there continue to be tense places, imagine this healing breath moving directly to those spots ... unknotting the tension... letting go ... letting be ... letting open ... letting unlock ...

As you give yourself the gift of relaxation, the gift of embodiment ... notice the inner space created by this letting go ... Notice how much this tension that has built up in you had been blocking your inner life ... your core-self ... how much it has been keeping you from being in touch with your sacred centre ... As your prepare this space, know that there is nowhere more important to be ... that there is nothing more important to do ... than to be present ... to yourself ... to the Holy Presence ... to the Spirit ... to your deep silent centre ...

Imagine yourself in a sacred place ... It is a safe place ... a place you and the Holy choose to meet ... It is a healing place ... an empowering place ... It is a space where you can encounter the Holy ... and the Sacred Presence can encounter you ... Notice the colours ... the sights ... the textures ... the sounds ... the smells ... Are there others with you in this place or are you alone? ...

Imagine yourself in the presence of a Spirit of unconditional love ... a Holy Presence ... What is this Presence like for you? ... How does it feel for you to be there? ... Can you allow yourself to ask for what you need ... what you desire most from God? ... What do you ask for? ... How does it feel to ask? ... What does the Holy Presence do? ... What response do you receive? ...

Imagine the Spirit offering you even more than you asked for ... Allow the Spirit to pour into you the spirit of wisdom and the spirit of insight so that you can know God more clearly ... Let it bathe your mind and all your thought patterns ... Let it bathe your memories ... and all your systems for looking at life ... Let it bathe your body ... Let it bathe your emotions ... Let it bathe your soul ... Let the spirit of wisdom and insight pour through every part of your being as a spiritual gift from God ...

Now imagine the Spirit giving you another spiritual gift ... the gift of opening your inner eyes so that you may be able to see deeply the hope for which you were created by God ... Get in touch with yourself as having been created by God who breathed God's hope into you ... allow the hope of God for you to be breathed into you ... Let it bathe your mind and all your thought patterns ... Let it bathe your memories ... and all your systems for looking at life ... Let it bathe your body ... Let it bathe your emotions ... Let it bathe your soul ... Let the hope for which you were created by God pour through every part of your being as a spiritual gift from God ... and let your inner eyes ... your inner vision ... be able to see that ... to feel that ... to know that hope ...

Now imagine the Spirit giving you another gift ... the gift of the power and strength of bringing life out of death ... the power to create and renew life in the face of death ... the power of Christ's resurrection ... new life for us ... Imagine this incredible life-creating ... life-renewing ... "life-in-the-face-of-death" power pouring into you ... Let it bathe your memories ... and all your systems for looking at life ... Let it bathe your body ... Let it bathe your emotions ... Let it bathe your soul ... Let the power of resurrection life pour through every part of your being as a spiritual gift from God ...

Meditation 21

Know that these spiritual gifts are yours ... They are given to you not just for this moment ... but for always ... They are gifts you can access whenever you need them ... Say thank you to the Spirit ... and make whatever closure feels right for you ...

Let yourself gradually and gently be drawn back to this place ... Become aware of your breath ... of your body-self ... Begin to make some gentle movements with your toes and fingers ... some rolls of your head and shoulders ... as you draw yourself back to this place and open your eyes.

SHARING
JOURNALLING/DRAWING

DEBRIEFING
Invite participants to share what they feel comfortable sharing from the experience of the meditation. You may wish to have the scripture copied for the participants to take home with them. I particularly like the paraphrase of this passage in Eugene Peterson's *The Message* .

CLOSURE
Sing: God is Passionate Life

22

COMFORT, O COMFORT MY PEOPLE
AN ADVENT MEDITATION

INTRODUCTION

PREPARATION
- paper and pens/pencils/drawing materials
- questions for debriefing on flip chart for journalling
- a cloth
- candle
- open Bible

SCRIPTURE: ISAIAH 40:1–11

REFLECTION

Advent is a season to prepare for the radical transformation that comes with incarnation. Most of us find it impossible to believe that we are really worthy, or able to incarnate the presence of God. Advent reminds us that with God the impossible becomes possible, and the normal rules of power and might do not apply. God works with what seems unlikely in the culture's power structure. Holy birth is to come through an ordinary peasant woman. A defeated people in captivity in some God-forsaken land are not forgotten, but are called to be a vehicle of promise.

This scripture addresses a broken people who feel abandoned by God. A deep sense of hopelessness and powerlessness sucks life out of the people. They feel nothing can change; that they are simply victims of those with more military strength. God's voice of tenderness and comfort (from the Latin *cum*, "with" and *fortis*, "strength") comes to the people in the midst of their captivity, in the midst of their exile, telling them to prepare a way for God in the wilderness.

The wilderness was a place of danger, a place to be dreaded, a place where one could become lost or even die. Moses had led the Israelite slaves out from Egypt in search of a promised land. They had spent forty long years wandering in the wilderness before they arrived in the good land of promise. There had been sustenance when they least expected it. There had been water in impossible places. This had been a time of toughening and of formation for the people. Yet the idea of going out into the desert again, even from the dislocation of exile in Babylon, might not have had a lot of appeal.

God's promise comes right into the core of the powerlessness, and proclaims that the people have a mission — to prepare God's way in the wilderness — to literally be part of changing the terrain — lifting up valleys, bringing down mountains, making rough places plain. And when this happens, God's living presence (the glory of God was the way it was expressed in scripture) will be seen to be with the people and they will find the power to cry out, even though they lack confidence in themselves and feel they do not know what to say. God will gentle and strengthen them to find their voice and their power. God will enable them to climb high mountains, to speak with a voice of strength, to be messengers of good news, to lift up their voices without fear, to proclaim hope to the culture.

Surely this is a message we need to embody, and en-flesh in these times of drowning in despair and powerlessness at the enormity of the problems and pain of our world.

GATHERING

a)   Be in touch with a time you felt in exile as did the Israelites to whom these words were spoken:
   - What are the feelings associated with that time in your life?
   - What helped you move out of it (if you did)?
   - What did you need to hear in that time? Did this happen for you or not?
   - What word of comfort do you still need to hear from God? From others?

b)   When you think of these times in our world, where do you feel the sense of exile, of rootlessness, of dislocation, of being overpowered by the strong? Where do you hear God's call to be strong, to take on the power, to cry out with strength, to prepare a way?

c)   The Israelites were in captivity to an oppressing power. But they were also in captivity to their despair, and to their old images of God, and how God should have acted to save them.
   - To what do you feel we are in captivity as a culture? As individuals?

d) Through the prophet, God speaks of the way that must be prepared in the wilderness. Valleys are to be uplifted. Mountains and hills are to be brought low. Rough spots are to be smoothed. How does this connect with where you are in your journey now?

e) Finding the power to speak out because of comfort received seems to be the dynamic of this passage:
   - How are you at receiving comfort and tenderness from the presence of God? Are you able to ask? Are you able to receive?
   - How are you at transforming the assurance and grace into action?
   - What are the issues that you need to raise your voice and speak out about?

MEDITATION

Shut your eyes and let your body relax ... Let it sink into the chair or into the floor ... Let yourself be held up ... supported by the chair or floor ... You do not need to do the work of holding up your body ... You can let it be supported ... You can let go and relax ...

Begin to notice your breathing ... Breath is essential to living ... It was God's breath, we are told, that created all that is ... It has the power for cleansing and healing not only our physical system ... but also our emotional and spiritual lives ... Notice the breath as it begins at the tip of your nose ... Feel the cool air as it moves through your nostrils ... Follow it as it moves across the roof of your mouth ... Follow it as it goes down into your windpipe ... Follow it as it goes through your bronchial tubes into your lungs ... Notice where it goes into your lungs ... How deeply is the breath of life moving within you? ...

Gradually allow your breath to move more deeply into your being ... Let it open up space inside you ... space to meet the Holy ... space for you to BE ...

Gradually allow yourself to soften and flow with the breath ... Let your shoulders fall and relax as you breathe into the part of your lungs high up in your shoulders ... Let your tummy muscles relax and let go as you let the breath move deeply into your whole torso ... Notice what it feels like to be in your body-self as this happens ... Notice the feeling of letting go ... of relaxing ... of well-being ... of inner space for meeting the Holy ...

Pick one place (either the tip of the nose or a place in the lungs) in which to simply observe the breath as it passes ... in and out ... in and out ... Let yourself come to your sacred centre to the still place inside ...

The Israelites were in a place in Babylon where they were not in a lot of physical danger, but a place where they were not at home ... a place where they did not have a free choice to leave ... a place where they did not have roots or connections. In your imagination, enter Babylon as one of the exiles ... Feel the heat of the place ... the desert sun ... the sand in the air when the wind blows ... Feel the foreignness of the place ... The sense that you do not belong here ... You are a stranger in a strange land ...

Feel the sense that there is nothing you can do to change the situation ... Your institutions are not allowed ... It is difficult to meet with others who have had the same experience as you ... You feel isolated ... You have enough to eat, and you are not a slave, but you are not free either ... and your soul is starving for the stories of your people ... for the stories of your God ... for stories from home, and how it used to be when Yahweh was with us ... Feel your longing for roots ...

Feel also the sense of confusion around God ... When you were home in Jerusalem, you knew that God's glory, the presence of God was in the Holy of Holies in the temple ... a place you could never approach ... And you always had heard that Israel was God's chosen nation ... that God was on your side ... So how do you deal with military defeat ... with the destruction of the temple, including the Holy of Holies ... with being forced to march across the desert to this foreign land ... no time to find all your family members ... no time to say good-bye ... no time to prepare and to take the things that mattered ...

And now you are here ... And what is to become of you?...

You hear that someone is going to come today who is a messenger from God ... You hear others talking about it ... In the past God's prophets had come with messages of doom, and warnings of destruction if there were not some radical changes in the society ... No one believed them then ... Yet look what had happened ... You wonder if you really want to go to hear this one now ...

Down by the river in the afternoon while the others are sleeping everyone can come and hear ... How do you feel about this invitation? ... Imagine yourself gathering with the others near the river ... At least the air feels cooler beside the lazy water ... Notice the others who are there ... What are the feelings in you and in the others as you await the arrival of the prophet of God? ...

You become aware that this one you were waiting for has arrived ... What kind of person do you see? ... As the prophet begins to speak, it is as if God were speaking directly through that person ... Allow these words to speak to your soul ...

Comfort ... O comfort my people ... Allow yourself to let those words sink into your whole being ... like healing oils in wounded places ... like gentle massage in knotted places ... As the word comfort comes, allow the experience of comfort ... of healing ... of coming with strength... to pour into you ... to pour through you ... Feel the presence of the Holy One who wants to speak and be comfort and tenderness to you ...

Now be yourself in this place by the river ... In your own sense of exile ... of un-freedom ... of captivity ... in your own feelings of abandonment ... of powerless ... let the experience of God's comfort permeate like gently falling rain into thirsty ground ... Where do you need that healing strength in your life right now? ... Can you let yourself receive it from a tender God ... a God who wants to be with you with gentle healing power? ...

And then into the place where you feel you have no power ... where you feel you have lost any meaning or direction for your life ... hear the Holy One's messenger ... inviting and challenging you to prepare a sacred way in the wilderness ... in the very place that you have avoided ... in the very place you have feared ...

What does preparing a sacred way in the wilderness, in the desert mean for you right now? ... What would preparing a way mean in your desert? ... What would God's way look like in the desert you experience in your personal life? ... in the life of your community? ... in the life of the planet?...

Take one of these areas that connects with you now, and take some time to imagine the way being prepared ... Obstacles being brought low ... Valleys being lifted up ... Rough rocky places being smoothed ... And there is in all of this a profound sense of the transforming living presence of the Holy One ... Feel the turmoil ... feel the change ... feel the upside-down power of this God ... as the Spirit works to create a way through the desert ... as it works to restore ... to reconcile ... to create a just way ... Be in touch with this powerful energy for transformation ... this energy that can meet you in the desert where you feel you have no hope, no power ...

Let it kindle again the flames of life within ... Israel was called to cry out! ... not to suffer in silence, not to be passive victims ... They were called to break out of their despondent feeling that nothing was worth it ... that nothing could change ... They were called to go up to a high mountain ... to lift up their voices with strength ... to find their voice ... to speak their truth ... to bring good news ... to bring hope and possibility and promise ... And they are told not to be afraid to do this ... They were to proclaim that God is alive and in their midst with caring and empowerment ...

As you spend time with this messenger of God, is there a call that comes for you? ... Is there a place where you are challenged to speak out? ... Is there a place where you are being invited to move from powerlessness to finding your voice? ... If you found your voice to cry out the Spirit's good news, what might you say? ... Can you feel the invitation not to fear? ... Can you feel the call to be with strength? ... Can you imagine the deserts in your own life experience being turned upside down? ... Can you imagine yourself preparing a way? ...

Is there some particular part of this invitation that you feel you want to
work with in this season of advent? ... What help would you need to be able
to do this? ... Can you ask for it? ... If there are any things that you need to
ask or to say to the messenger, let yourself do this now as you prepare to
leave and return to this place ...

When you are ready, reconnect with your breathing ... gently make some
movements with your toes and fingers and shoulders as you reconnect with
your body and gently, gradually prepare to return ... Open your eyes when
you feel ready.

SHARING

JOURNALLING/DRAWING
Have the debriefing questions prepared on a flip chart and invite participants to
journal before sharing.

DEBRIEFING
Share in twos to help integrate the insights received in meditation. Share with the
whole group, as appropriate in your own setting:
- What are one or two aspects of this meditation experience that call to you
as a challenge to grow?
- What do you need in order to do this? from others? from yourself? from
God?
- What first step do you feel compelled to take right now?

CLOSURE

A circle prayer, where each person is invited to name the challenge they received,
and what they need from others or from God.

23

ROLLING THE STONES AWAY
A MEDITATION FOR EASTER

INTRODUCTION

PREPARATION

- paper and pens/pencils/drawing materials
- candle
- open Bible
- large stone
- container to symbolize the spices the women were bringing to the tomb
- basket of smaller stones to offer to participants at the closure to help them remember the stones they are rolling away

SCRIPTURE: MARK 16:1–6

REFLECTION

Imagine the atmosphere in the days immediately following Jesus' death. The women who had stayed with Jesus through the horror of his execution on the Roman cross, now brave the danger of going to care for the body of the One who had been their leader and friend. Everywhere the atmosphere is tense; the whole country is a political powder keg.

Roman occupiers of the Jewish nation of Palestine are anxious about the large numbers of tourists and pilgrims in town because of the Passover. Many have come from Galilee, the area they believed was teeming with sedition and rebellion. Jesus was not the first Galilean they had executed to make a point. The historian Josephus tells us that there had been a chain of executions of rebels, particularly from Galilee, which was a region where the opposition to Rome seemed to be centred. All the wars of independence seemed to begin there.[19]

This helps us understand Peter's fear to admit to being with the Galilean when he was confronted. It also helps to understand the fear and danger the disciples felt when they were hidden away in locked rooms after the crucifixion. No wonder most of them scattered in terror when Jesus was arrested.

It must have been an extreme act of courage for Jesus' mother Mary, and for the other women who were followers and friends of Jesus, to stay throughout the torture. And to venture forth on this morning to find and care for the body of this One whom they had loved was also a courage-filled act in the face of great danger.

How often, around the world, when women to do the simple ordinary acts of living, raising children, trying to create safe homes, caring for those who have died they face hardship and danger. There are many stones that need to be rolled away for fullness of life to emerge. No wonder this image was a central image in the Ecumenical Decade of Churches in Solidarity with Women.

GATHERING

a)   Introduce the scripture and read it slowly.

b)   Ask participants to think about what stones they might name that keep them walled in the stony, silent place of un-living; stones that are blocking new life for them? Give them time to write these down and invite them to share (with one other or the whole group, according to the nature and size of your group).

MEDITATION

Shut your eyes ... let yourself begin to connect with this body-self that you are ... this holy temple ... Many of us spend our whole lives disconnected from our body-self ... We take our body for granted ... We do not recognize it as created in God's image ... as a source of wisdom and profound knowing ... Ask your body to teach you its wisdom as your relax ... as you tell your mind that it doesn't need to help you for the next while ... that it is good for you to relax and just be for the next little while ... Tell your mind that it can take a rest ... that you appreciate that it is trying to help, but that just for now you want to be fully present to your body-self ... and to its wisdom ...

As you begin to pay attention to your body, do you notice places where tension is stored up? ... where your muscles are in tight knots? ... As you scan your body, from the top of your head to the bottom of your feet ... notice if there are tender places ... sore spots ... and send compassion to these places in your body, thanking them for the hard work they are doing ... perhaps offering to pay more attention to what they are telling you in the future ... Befriend the places of pain in your body...

Become aware of your breathing ... of the life-sustaining breath that goes on all of the time ... even when we are unaware ... Notice if you are breathing with only a small part of your lungs, or whether you are taking the breath deeply into your whole being ... down to the bottom of your lungs ... Breathe with your whole torso ... your whole body... Take the breath of life up to the tops of your shoulders ... a place where many of us store stress and the heavy loads we are carrying ... Notice if your tummy moves in and out as you inhale and exhale ... the way a baby's does when it is breathing naturally ...

Notice where you are tightened up ... not fully open to the breath of life ... Let your body relax ... let the tension flow out of your body through your feet ... Begin to allow your breath to move deeper into your being ... taking the breath deep down into your belly ... creating inner space ... Breathe in deeply the healing presence of the Spirit ... the goodness and grace of God ... Take it right into your centre ...

With each breath out, allow the breath to carry away the toxins that have built up ... the physical poisons that need to be cleansed ... Let it also carry out the emotional poisons that have been stored in your body ... the pains and angers that need to be let go ... Let the healing breath gently caress the wounded places ... let the life-giving breath of God work in a healing, cleansing way in your body-self ... in your emotional-self ... in your spirit-self ... Let the rhythm of taking in newness and healing ... and letting go of built-up tensions and stress ... take root in this time of meditation ... Know that this is a force for deep inner healing that is planted in you by the Creator ... and that this is a power you may access whenever you want, or

need to ... The breath keeps your body open ... allowing it to do its work ...
allowing the energies to flow ...

Breathe in possibility ... Breathe in the hope that the Spirit gives ... Let go of
the stress and tensions that are stored in your body-self ... and in your
emotional-self ... and in your spiritual-self ... Breathe in life energy ... The
creating breath of God that was there from the beginning ... Breathe out
whatever would block you from being fully present to this time ... Again
notice your body ... If there continue to be tense places, imagine this healing breath moving directly to those spots ... unknotting the tension ...
letting go ... letting be ... letting open ... letting unlock ...

As you give yourself the gift of relaxation, the gift of embodiment ... notice
the inner space created by this letting go ... Notice how much this tension
that has built up in you had been blocking your inner life ... your core-self
... how much it has been keeping you from being in touch with your sacred
centre ... As your prepare this space, know that there is nowhere more
important to be ... that there is nothing more important to do ... than to be
present ... to yourself ... to the Holy Presence ... to the Spirit ... to your deep
silent centre ...

In your imagination ... get a sense of being sealed in a dark cave hollowed
out of the side of a hill ... There is a stone that is blocking the entrance
way ...

Get an image of the stone that keeps you walled in the stony silent place of
un-living ... the stone that blocks the way to the light and freedom of life in
all its fullness ... the stone that blocks out the fresh air ... that keeps us just
breathing and recycling the same old stuff over and over again ...

Reflect on your own life now ... your personal life ... but also your life in
community ... your life in a larger world ... In your mind's eye ... let the
Spirit show you those stony walls that stifle alive-ness ... stones that block
your way to communion with God ... stones that block your creativity ...
stones that block your living-ness ... your being fully alive to be all that God
intends you to be ...

Allow the Spirit to show you some of the stones that block life in all its fullness for others ... for the world God loves ... Take the time you need to allow the Spirit to connect you with those stones that you can see most clearly at this time ...

Let yourself also connect with the call of the Spirit to come to life ... to come out from the tomb ... Feel the breath of the Spirit pour into your whole being ... Allow the feeling for being alive ... the call to life ... to awaken your soul ... your body-self ... Feel the newness of life come into you almost as if you were being created anew ... Allow that energy for life to rise up in you ... to give you strength ... to give you the power to roll away the stones that keep you locked up and that prevent living ...

Imagine the struggle to roll the stone away ... the resistance of the heavy stone to leaving the place in which it has been set ... Feel the power of life giving you the strength and the persistence to keep moving the stone ... Notice the first glimmer of light that penetrates the darkness ... Savour that light ... Allow that light to fill you with a desire for more ... Notice the first fresh air that comes into the cave ... Feel the goodness of breathing fresh air ... and let that first breath of air fill you with the promise and desire for more ... Now with renewed strength, because you have tasted the possibility of freedom ... allow every ounce of your strength to roll the stone away ... and allow yourself to experience freedom from imprisonment ...

Breathe the air ... Savour the light ... Feel the freedom ... Feel the possibility and the promise ... Feel the call to begin again in power ... What does it now mean for you to be fully alive? ... How will it change your life? ... Take all the time you need to experience this new life ...

Let yourself gradually and gently draw yourself back to this place ... Become aware of your breath ... of your body-self ... Begin to make some gentle movements with your toes and fingers ... some rolls of your head and shoulders as you draw yourself back to this place and open your eyes.

SHARING

JOURNALLING/DRAWING

DEBRIEFING
Invite participants to share what they feel comfortable sharing from the experience of the meditation.

CLOSURE

a)   If you have a basket of stones, you might invite participants to choose one to remind them of their meditation experience.

b)   Sing: God is Passionate Life.

ROLLING THE STONES AWAY:
A RITUAL FOR WORSHIP

I have used this after an abbreviated version of the previous meditation at worship on Easter Sunday.[20] Our liturgical dancers moved large stones I had placed on the communion table and placed them in baskets that they took away at the end of the ritual. As they carried the baskets down the aisles, we invited worshippers to place (in the baskets) the stones they wished to roll away symbolically.

MEDITATION
(as above)

One: Let us also connect with the call of God's Spirit to come to life — to come out from the tomb. Let us allow the energy for life to rise up in us, to give us the power to roll away the stones that prevent us from living. Think of your own stones that block fullness of life for you, for the community, for the world as I name some that may or may not include the ones you are thinking of.

One: Fear. This stone is a difficult one to move, because it keeps us paralyzed, or makes us run away. Let us roll away the stone of the fear that binds us, as we remember that love casts out fear — as we learn to trust — and to act in spite of being afraid. We need to learn to act when we are afraid — just as we have learned to act when we are tired.[21]

One: Let us roll away this stone that blocks abundant living.

All: **The stone is rolled away. Christ is risen, Hallelujah!**

One: Powerlessness. This stone is like fear for it immobilizes us from taking on our lives. This stone keeps us cut off from our Sacred Source. It keeps us locked in the victim role. It keeps us from accessing the sacred right that is ours as people of God. Let us roll away the stone of powerlessness, and feel the freedom and perhaps also the anxiety of empowerment.

One: Let us roll away this stone that blocks abundant living.

All: **The stone is rolled away. Christ is risen, Hallelujah!**

One: Alienation. This stone keeps us lonely, neglected and neglecting. It keeps us from belonging and from inviting others to belong. Let us roll away the stone of alienation in our lives:
- as we dare to trust,
- as we dare to let others in to share our journey,
- as we dare to reach out to others on this spiritual path.

One: Let us roll away this stone that blocks abundant living.

All: **The stone is rolled away. Christ is risen, Hallelujah!**

One: Discrimination. This stone comes in many forms and is often used for throwing or for crushing. Its name is sexism, its name is racism, its name is homophobia, its name is ageism, its name is class-ism. Wherever people are put in boxes and labelled, and treated through that box, rather than as the unique, sacred gift that they are, potential life is snuffed out, and abundant life is denied and distorted.

One: Let us roll away this stone that blocks abundant living.

All: **The stone is rolled away. Christ is risen, Hallelujah!**

One: Addiction. This stone is called addiction, and can come in many forms as well. Substance addiction, work addiction, addiction to perfection. Its promises are empty and hollow and it robs our life of meaning.

One: Let us roll away this stone that blocks abundant living.

All: **The stone is rolled away. Christ is risen, Hallelujah!**

One: Violence. It can be physical or emotional, but in both cases it destroys life in all its fullness. This stone destroys communities, homes, trusting relationships, children. It crushes the human spirit. Let us roll it away as we work in ourselves and in our world for zero tolerance level of violence — as we work for a safer, peaceful world.

One: Let us roll away this stone that blocks abundant living.

All: **The stone is rolled away. Christ is risen, Hallelujah!**

One: Consumerism. This stone is called consumerism. It fills us with the hollow promise that possessions will make us secure and happy. It dulls our response to the cries of the world. It leaves us ever-grasping and never satisfied. It is at the heart of economic systems that suggest that the rich have too little and the poor have too much. It makes a God of the profit margin, of the bottom line, and forgets people who are affected and community that is damaged. It renders voiceless the weak, the disabled, the poor, the unemployed. It strips away their God-given dignity.

One: Let us roll away this stone that blocks abundant living.

All: **The stone is rolled away. Christ is risen, Hallelujah!**

One: As we remove these stones that block us from communion with God and with one another, and with our deepest selves, let us embrace the space and freedom that come with letting go. Let us invite the resurrected life of the risen Christ to be alive in us, Eastering in us. Amen.

NOTES

◆•◆•◆

[1] A notable exception is by Carolyn Stahl, *Opening to God* (Nashville: The Upper Room, 1977). A more recent resource by Thomas A. Droege, *The Healing Presence* (San Francisco: HarperSanFrancisco, 1992) is also excellent but almost impossible to find.

[2] Other such disciplines might include journal writing, contemplative prayer, mantra meditation (one can use Biblical phrases if one chooses), body work, dream work, and chanting.

[3] Morton Kelsey in his book *Companions on the Inner Way, The Art of Spiritual Guidance* (New York: The Crossroad Publishing Company, 1983) has four chapters at the beginning of his book that offer a fuller history of the development of the western Christian spiritual tradition. Chapter two has a clear, concise analysis of the similarities and differences in world-view of eastern and western meditation practice. These chapters are The Spiritual Journey, Spiritual Guidance and the Western World, What is Mature Christianity? and The Christian Tradition.

[4] Henri J.M. Nouwen, *The Way of the Heart* (New York: Bantam Books, 1985)

[5] Dom John Mains died in 1982. The Christian meditation network founded on his teachings continues at Unitas, in Montreal, now an ecumenical spiritual centre, of which the United Church is also a sponsor.

[6] The work of O. Carl Simonton, Stephanie Matthews-Simonton, and James Creighton with cancer patients is outlined in *Getting Well Again* (New York: Bantam Books, 1980). Dr. Bernie S. Siegel, another cancer specialist, has written in this area as well in *Love, Medicine & Miracles* (New York: Harper and Row, 1986) and *Peace, Love and Healing* (New York: Harper and Row, 1989). Dr. Joan Borysenko deals with links between body and mind in healing in *Guilt is the Teacher, Love is the Lesson* (New York: Warner Books, 1990) and *Minding the Body, Mending the Mind* (New York: Bantam Books, 1988). Dr. Larry Dossey has written extensively about this in *Healing Words: The Power of Prayer and the Practice of Medicine* (San Francisco: HarperSanFrancisco, 1993) and *Recovering the Soul* (New York: Bantam Books, 1989).

Notes

Dr. Carl Jung, *Man and his Symbols* (New York: Doubleday, 1964).

John 3:8.

Claudio Naranjo, cited in David Fontana, *The Meditator's Handbook: Comprehensive Guide to Eastern and Western Meditation Techniques* (Rockport, MA: Element, 1992).

Carolyn Stahl, *Opening to God: Guided Imagery Meditation on Scripture for Individuals and Groups* (Nashville: The Upper Room, 1977)

One of the best is Ad de Vries, *Dictionary of Symbols and Imagery* (New York: North-Holland Publishing Co., 1984).

John 1:1–14

See note 3

See note 3

"Magnificat of Waiting" by Ann Johnson in *Miryam of Nazareth: Woman of Strength & Wisdom* (Notre Dame, IN: Ave Maria Press, 1984)

John Sanford, *Mystical Christianity: A Psychological Commentary on the Gospel of John* (New York: Crossroads, 1994)

Adapted from *Divine Light Invocation* by S. Radha, source unknown.

Eugene H. Peterson, *The Message* (Colorado Springs: Navpress, 1993)

See Chapter 7, "Good Friday" by Uta Ranke-Heinemann in *Putting Away Childish Things* (San Francisco: HarperSanFrancisco, 1994)

The idea for this liturgy is based on Communion Prayers prepared by Gisele Grifillan and a worship planning team of Queen's Theological College, Kingston, Ontario. The original was printed in *Gathering-Lent, Easter, Pentecost*, 1996.

I first heard this expression used by Charlotte Caron who was guest speaker at a Women In Ministry Conference in Ste Anne de Bellevue, Bellevue, Quebec.

BIBLIOGRAPHY

Some of these books may be out-of-print. You may find them in a church, theological college, or public library.

Augsburger, David, *Caring Enough to Forgive/Caring Enough to Not Forgive* (Scottdale, Pa: Herald Press, 1981)

Barry, William A., S.J., *Seek My Face* (New York: Paulist Press, 1989)

Bolen, Jean Shinoda, *The Tao of Psychology: Synchronicity and the Self* (San Francisco: Harper & Row, 1979)

Bonheim, Jalaja, *The Serpent and the Wave: A Guide to Movement Meditation* (Berkeley: Celestial Arts, 1992)

Borysenko, Joan, *Guilt is the Teacher, Love is the Lesson* (New York: Warner Books, 1990)

——, *Minding the Body, Mending the Mind* (New York: Bantam Books, 1988)

Brueggemann, Walter, *Living Toward a Vision - Biblical Reflections on Shalom* (New York: United Church Press, 1976)

Cooper, Joan, *Guided Meditation and the Teaching of Jesus* (Longmead, UK: Element Books, 1982)

de Mello, Anthony, *Wellsprings: A Book of Spiritual Exercises* (Garden City, NJ: Image Books, 1986)

de Vries, Ad, *Dictionary of Symbols and Imagery* (New York: North-Holland Publishing Co., l984)

Dossey, Larry, *Healing Words: The Power of Prayer and the Practice of Medicine* (San Francisco: HarperSanFrancisco, 1993)

——, *Recovering the Soul* (New York: Bantam Books, 1989)

Douglas-Klotz, Neil, *Desert Wisdom: Sacred Middle Eastern Writings from the Goddess through the Sufis* (San Francisco: HarperSanFrancisco, 1995)

Droege, Thomas A., *Guided Grief Imagery: A Resource for Grief Ministry and Death Education* (New York: Paulist Press, 1987)

Droege, Thomas A., *The Healing Presence* (San Francisco: HarperSanFrancisco, 1992)

Estés, Clarissa Pinkola, *Women Who Run with the Wolves* (New York: Ballantyne Books, 1992)

Fischer, Kathleen, *Reclaiming the Connections - a Contemporary Spirituality* (Kansas City: Sheed & Ward, 1990)

——, *Women at the Well: Feminist Perspectives on Spiritual Direction* (New York: Paulist Press, 1988)

Fontana, David, *The Meditator's Handbook: Comprehensive Guide to Eastern and Western Meditation Techniques* (Rockport, Mass: Element, 1992)

Fox, Matthew, *Original Blessing* (Santa Fe, New Mexico: Bear & Company, 1983)

——, *A Spirituality Named Compassion and the Healing of the Global Village, Humpty Dumpty and Us* (Minneapolis: Winston Press, 1979)

Frankl, Viktor E., *Man's Search for Meaning* (New York: Touchstone, 1962)

——, *The Unconscious God: Psychotherapy and Theology* (New York: Simon & Schuster, 1975)

Gateley, Edwina, *I Hear a Seed Growing* (Trabuco Canyon, CA: Source Books, 1990)

Grant, W Harold, Magdala Thompson, and Thomas E. Clarke, *From Image to Likeness: a Jungian Path in the Gospel Journey* (New York: Paulist Press, 1983)

Houston, Jean, *Godseed: the Journey of Christ* (Amity, NY: Amity House, 1988)

Johnson, Ann, *Miryam of Nazareth: Woman of Strength & Wisdom* (Notre Dame, IN: Ave Maria Press, 1984)

Jung, Carl, *Man and his Symbols* (New York: Doubleday, 1964)

Kelsey, Morton, *Companions on the Inner Way: the Art of Spiritual Guidance* (New York: Crossroad, 1983)

——, *The Other Side of Silence: A Guide to Christian Meditation* (Mahwah, NJ: Paulist Press, 1976)

Kolbenschlag, Madonna, *Lost in the Land of Oz: Befriending your Inner Orphan and Heading Home* (San Francisco: Harper & Row, 1988)

Leonard, Linda Schierse, *The Wounded Woman: Healing the Father-Daughter Relationship* (Boston: Shambhala, 1985)

Linn, Dennis, and Matthew Linn, *Healing Life's Hurts: Healing Memories Through the Five Stages of Forgiveness* (New York, Paulist Press, 1978)

Mariechild, Diane, *Crystal Visions: Nine Meditations for Personal and Planetary Peace* (Trumansburg, NY: The Crossing Press, 1985)

———, *The Inner Dance: a Guide to Spiritual and Psychological Unfolding* (Freedom, CA: The Crossing Press, 1987)

———, *Mother Wit, Feminist Guide to Psychic Development* (Trumansburg, NY: The Crossing Press, 1981)

Moore, Thomas, *Care of the Soul: A Guide for Cultivating Depth and Sacredness in Everyday Life* (New York: HarperPerennial, 1992)

Morton, Nelle, *The Journey is Home* (Boston: Beacon Press, 1985)

Nouwen, Henri J. M., *Life of the Beloved: Spiritual Living in a Secular World* (New York: Crossroad, 1995)

O'Connor, Elizabeth *Eighth Day of Creation: Discovering Your Gifts and Using Them* (Waco: Word Books, 1971)

———, *Journey Inward, Journey Outward* (San Francisco: Harper San Francisco, 1975)

Peck, M. Scott, *The Road Less Traveled: A New Psychology of Love, Traditional Values and Spiritual Growth* (New York: Touchstone, 1978)

Peterson, Eugene H., *The Message* (Colorado Springs: Navpress, 1993)

Plaskow, Judith, and Carol P. Christ, *Weaving the Visions: New Patterns in Feminist Spirituality* (San Francisco: Harper & Row, 1989)

Powers, Isaias, *Quiet Places with Jesus: 46 Guided Imagery Meditations for Personal Prayer* (Mystic, CT: Twenty-third Publications, 1978)

Ranke-Heinemann, Uta, *Putting Away Childish Things* (San Francisco: HarperSanFrancisco, 1994)

Rupp, Joyce, *Dear Heart, Come Home: The Path of Midlife Spirituality* (New York: A Croossroad Book, 1996)

——, *May I Have this Dance?* (Notre Dame: Ave Maria Press, 1992)

Sanford, John, *Healing and Wholeness* (New York: Paulist Press, 1971)

—— *Mystical Christianity: A Psychological Commentary on the Gospel of John* (New York: Crossroads, 1994)

Santa-Maria, Maria L., *Growth Through Meditation and Journal Writing: A Jungian Perspective on Christian Spirituality* (New York: Paulist Press, 1983)

Siegel, Bernie S., *Love, Medicine & Miracles* (New York: Harper and Row, 1986)

——, *Peace, Love and Healing* (New York: Harper and Row, 1989)

Simonton, O. Carl, Stephanie Matthews-Simonton, and James Creighton, *Getting Well Again* (New York: Bantam Books, 1980)

Soëlle, Dorothy, *The Inward Road and the Way Back* (London: Darton, Longman & Todd, 1979)

Stahl, Carolyn, *Opening to God: Guided Imagery Meditation on Scripture for Individuals and Groups* (Nashville: The Upper Room, 1977)

Steinem, Gloria, *Revolution from Within: A Book of Self-esteem* (Boston: Little, Brown and Company, 1992)

Stringfellow, William, *An Ethic for Christians & Other Aliens in a Strange Land* (Waco: Word Books, 1973)

——, *The Politics of Spirituality* (Philadelphia: The Westminster Press, 1984)

Teilhard de Chardin, Pierre, *Le Milieu Divin* (London & Glasgow: Fontana, 1964)

Wink, Walter, *The Bible and Human Transformation* (Philadelphia: Fortress Press, 1973)

——, *Transforming Bible Study* (Nashville: Abingdon, 1980)

Wuellner, Flora S., *Prayer and our Bodies* (Nashville: The Upper Room, 1987)

——, *Prayer, Stress, and Our Inner Wounds* (Nashville: The Upper Room, 1985)

Yungblut, John R., *Discovering God Within* (Philadelphia: The Westminster Press, 1979)

Zimmer, Mary, *Sister Images: Guided Meditations from the Stories of Biblical Women* (Nashville: Abingdon Press, 1993)

SCRIPTURE INDEX

Song Index

Unless otherwise noted, the music selections are from *Voices United*

Voices United: The Hymn and Worship Book of The United Church of Canada, John Ambrose, ed.
(Etobicoke, ON: United Church Publishing House, 1996).